JUSTIN BIEBER

Oh Baby!

MARY BOONE

TRIUMPH
BOOKS

Triumph Books and colophon are registered trademarks of Random House, Inc.

This book is available in quantity at special discounts for your group or
organization. For further information, contact:
Triumph Books
542 South Dearborn Street
Suite 750
Chicago, Illinois 60605
(312) 939-3330
Fax (312) 663-3557
www.triumphbooks.com

Printed in U.S.A.
ISBN: 978-1-60078-539-9

Content developed and packaged by Rockett Media, Inc.
Writer: Mary Boone
Editor: Bob Baker
Design and page production: Stephanie Urban
Cover design: Paul Petrowsky

PHOTO: ASSOCIATED PRESS

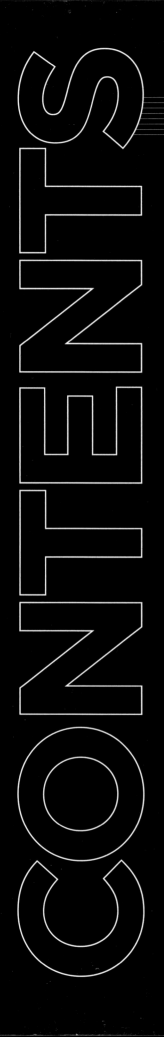

CONTENTS

JUSTIN

BIEBER

Chapter 1: Humble Beginnings

CHAPTER 1:
HUMBLE BEGINNINGS

Justin Bieber didn't take a normal path to pop-music stardom. He never modeled as a child. He didn't have a show on the Disney Channel. He didn't star in commercials for Jell-O or laundry detergent. He wasn't on *American Idol* or *America's Got Talent*. His family didn't pack up and move to Los Angeles in pursuit of an agent.

Nope. Justin didn't do the things pop stars before him have done. His story is extraordinary and, in the eyes of his growing legion of fans, so is his talent.

Justin Drew Bieber was born March 1, 1994, in Stratford, Ontario, Canada, to Pattie Mallette and Jeremy Bieber.

As a teenager, Pattie hoped to become an actress, but those dreams dissolved when she became pregnant at 18. She raised Justin alone, though he still is in touch with his father. Pattie worked two jobs just to keep the bills paid. Money wasn't plentiful, but love and good times were. Justin remembers a childhood filled with laughter, family and music. Rhythm and blues tunes often blared from the home's stereo, and spontaneous dancing was known to occur.

"We were living below the poverty line," Mallette told *Entertainment Weekly*. "We had a roof over our heads and we had food in the house, but we really struggled."

"I grew up with not a lot of money," Justin told *ABC News*. "I lived with mom. My mom and dad split up when I was very young. I had a relationship with my dad, but they were split up. So I was with my mom. Then I was with my dad.... I didn't have a lot of money, but I didn't know that."

Justin's musical career started simply enough – with a pair of drumsticks.

"My mom bought me my first drum kit when I was four because I was banging on everything around the house, even couches," he told *Billboard* magazine.

Determined to make the banging sound more like music, Justin practiced and practiced. He listened to music and tried to copy drum patterns he heard. His skills grew—and so did the list of instruments he could play.

"When he was five, he'd hear something on the radio and go to the keyboard and figure it out," his

" When I started playing the guitar, I picked up a **right-handed guitar** because that was all … my mom had."

JUSTIN BIEBER: *Oh Baby!*

mother, Pattie, told *Entertainment Weekly*. In addition to piano and drums, he also taught himself to play trumpet and guitar.

"At eight I started to play the guitar," Justin told ABC News. "Basically, when I started playing the guitar I picked up a right-handed guitar because that was all ... my mom had a right-handed guitar in the house. And (I) picked it up left-handed. My mom would switch it the other way and I would switch it right back to the other way and try to play. It was difficult because it's backwards."

Moved by her son's determination, Pattie saved up to buy young Justin a left-handed guitar for his next birthday. Having the right instrument made all the difference; Justin's frustration faded and his play-

Justin performs on CBS News' *The Early Show* in February 2010. Thousands of fans showed up for the show on Florida's famed Sound Beach.

PHOTO: CHRISTOPHER POLK/GETTY IMAGES

STRATFORD, ONTARIO, Canada

Stratford is a city of about 30,000 people that calls itself "Canada's Premier Arts Town." Now, it's also the proud hometown of pop star Justin Bieber.

Located in southwest Ontario, Canada, Stratford is about two hours from Toronto and three hours from Detroit, Michigan. The city has gained fame as home to the long-running Stratford Festival, a repertory theatre festival that's the largest of its kind in North America. Plays ranging from classic to contemporary are produced from April to November. The festival attracts audiences of more than 500,000 people each season and typically employs another 1,000.

When he was younger, Bieber liked to perform on the steps outside one of the four theatres that host the Stratford Festival. Appreciative tourists were happy to toss cash into his guitar case.

Stratford is so proud of its native son that the city recently posted a "Bieber-iffic Map to Stratford" on its website. The map (at www.welcometostratford.com/justin) guides folks past sites including:

Justin's Hometown

• Madelyn's Diner – Justin's favorite Stratford restaurant.
• King's Buffet – The location of Justin's first date.
• William Altman Memorial Arena – Where Justin's traveling hockey team played its home games.
• Cooper Standard Soccer Fields – Home turf for Justin's team, the Stratford Strikers.

The online map guides visitors past 16 of Justin's favorite places, but don't expect the tour to get too upclose and personal.

"We just had a family come in today to ask where Justin's house is and, of course, we couldn't tell them," said Shelby Van Klooster, who works for the Stratford Tourism Alliance. "We've got to respect his family's privacy you know."

Van Klooster says it's not uncommon for fan mail to come to Bieber with no address other than "Stratford, Ontario." When that happens, it's forwarded to the tourism office and bundled for delivery to Justin's grandparents.

"It's clear he has a lot of fans who love him," Van Klooster said. "What city wouldn't be proud of something like that?"

Justin Bieber performs at 102.7 KIIS-FM's Wango Tango 2010 show, held at the Staples Center on May 15, 2010, in Los Angeles, California.

ing improved.

Justin attended Stratford Northwest Secondary, a public school for students in grades 9-12. He was an average student who preferred English over science or math. By all accounts, his life was "normal."

> "He was **approachable**. He was **accessible**. He was **handsome** and **talented**. He was everything Braun thought he needed to be – except for one thing."

He dated a few girls, played center forward on his hockey team, cheered on the Toronto Maple Leafs, played chess, hung out with his friends, played golf, shot hoops, and skateboarded.

"Before, I was really concentrating on sports," Bieber told the *Toronto Star*. "I played hockey a lot. I was really focused on sports."

In 2007, he entered a local talent contest called Stratford Star. Modeled after the television show *American Idol*, contestants were judged in weekly competitions, until there were just a handful of finalists. While some others in the competition had extensive

music training, Justin wasn't so serious about singing at the time. In fact, most of his previous musical performances had taken place in front of his own bedroom mirror.

Still, Justin's energy and raw talent wowed the judges and

he ended up winning second place in the citywide contest.

Justifiably proud of his accomplishments, Justin wanted to share his victory with loved ones who weren't able to see him in person. He started posting his Stratford Star videos on YouTube, including a rendition of Aretha Franklin's "Respect." In the video, a 12-year-old Justin bounces and dances across the stage in an oversized brown, plaid shirt, his baseball cap on backwards. While the performance is far from professional – at one point he plays "air" saxophone and then drops the microphone onto the stage – Justin's enthusiasm and talent shine through.

His family liked the video; even his closest friends were surprised by his talent.

"I didn't tell my friends (I had entered the contest) because they didn't really know that I could sing," he told *Billboard*. "They knew me for playing sports. I just wanted to be a regular kid and I knew they wouldn't treat me the same way if I told them."

With his secret unveiled, Justin started posting more videos online. There was a clip of him rapping Lil Bow Wow's "Basketball" and one in which he's wearing a tie and dress shirt singing Ne-Yo's "So Sick." He's caught on tape in his bathroom singing "Back at One" by Brian McKnight and he sits on the sofa in another, strumming the guitar and singing Justin Timberlake's "Cry Me a River."

Justin says he's never tried to imitate a particular sound or artist.

"I would never try to be like anybody," he told *MacLeans*. "I definitely had people that I looked up to. I looked up to Michael Jackson and Stevie Wonder and Boyz II Men. But I never tried to sound like anybody."

While there are thousands of amateur videos of amateur singers on the Internet, Justin's somehow caught the attention of web-browsing tweens. They emailed links to the videos to friends, who sent them to friends, and soon Justin's YouTube videos went viral. By May 2010, his

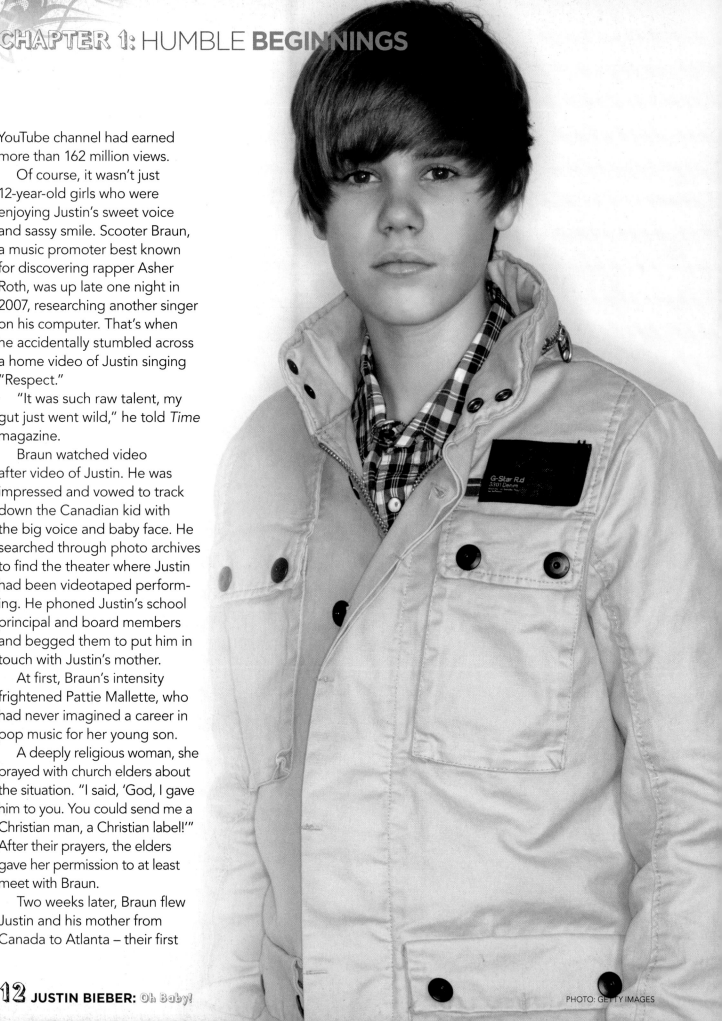

YouTube channel had earned more than 162 million views.

Of course, it wasn't just 12-year-old girls who were enjoying Justin's sweet voice and sassy smile. Scooter Braun, a music promoter best known for discovering rapper Asher Roth, was up late one night in 2007, researching another singer on his computer. That's when he accidentally stumbled across a home video of Justin singing "Respect."

"It was such raw talent, my gut just went wild," he told *Time* magazine.

Braun watched video after video of Justin. He was impressed and vowed to track down the Canadian kid with the big voice and baby face. He searched through photo archives to find the theater where Justin had been videotaped perform-ing. He phoned Justin's school principal and board members and begged them to put him in touch with Justin's mother.

At first, Braun's intensity frightened Pattie Mallette, who had never imagined a career in pop music for her young son.

A deeply religious woman, she prayed with church elders about the situation. "I said, 'God, I gave him to you. You could send me a Christian man, a Christian label!'" After their prayers, the elders gave her permission to at least meet with Braun.

Two weeks later, Braun flew Justin and his mother from Canada to Atlanta – their first

GETTING FAMOUS THANKS TO YOUTUBE

Pals Chad Hurley, Steve Chen and Jawed Karim started YouTube in 2005 as an easy way to upload and share videos with friends. They hoped others would like the website, but they couldn't

After internet fame, Lonelygirl15's *Jessica Rose* appeared on ABC Family's *Greek*

even have imagined how popular it would become. YouTube now averages nearly 20 million visitors per month.

Justin Bieber owes much of his sudden stardom to videos he posted on YouTube that quickly began attracting thousands of views and the attention of music industry executives. He's definitely a YouTube success story, but he's not the only celebrity to have gained fame via online

videos. A few others you may want to check out include:

Jessica Lee Rose (lonelygirl15)

In the summer of 2006, Rose debuted as *Lonelygirl15*, a fictional teen character named Bree. Initially, it was thought the videos were posted by a "real" blogger. The show was eventually proven to be fictional by reporters who identified Rose as an actress portraying the lead character. Rose went on to get parts in ABC Family's *Greek* and to appear in movies including *Perfect Sport* and SyFy's *Ghost Town*.

Lucas Cruikshank (Fred Figglehorn)

Cruikshank found his ticket to fame in Fred Figglehorn, a high-pitched, fast-talking, fictional 6-year-old. In 2009, Cruikshank's channel became the first YouTube channel to hit one million subscribers.

In 2010, Cruikshank will star in Nickelodeon's *Fred: The Movie*, a production based on his YouTube character.

Andy McKee (acoustic musician)

This Topeka, Kansas, native started posting videos of his music online in late 2006. His dedicated online community has since raised his YouTube video views to more than 78 million plays. His online success has led to a contract with Candyrat Records and he's now touring internationally, with more than 200 shows booked in 2010.

Adam Nyerere Bahner (also known as Tay Zonday)

Bahner was a Minnesota college student in 2007, when he posted his "Chocolate Rain" video on YouTube. By April 2010 the clip had more than 50 million views. Before long, Bahner was making guest appearances on *Jimmy Kimmel Live!* and was featured on the cover of the *Los Angeles Times* Sunday arts section. He landed a featured role in a Vizio Super Bowl commercial starring Beyonce Knowles and in a campaign to promote Cherry Chocolate Diet Dr. Pepper. He now supports himself by acting, singing and doing voiceover work.

flight ever. It was during that trip to Atlanta that Justin bumped into his idol, Usher, in the music studio parking lot. Justin eagerly offered to sing for Usher, who politely refused.

Justin was disappointed but not discouraged. He and his mom talked strategy with Braun. They made plans about the best ways to build a fan base, which

among other artists. Usher remembers seeing the videos.

"His voice was magical and his personality was so keen," he told the *New York Times*. "He just knew how to be."

But when Usher called Braun and asked to meet Justin, he was told to get in line.

"Scooter (Braun) said, 'Justin is interested in this kid,'" Usher

"His voice was magical and his personality was so keen. He just knew how to be."

labels to approach, and which songs best suited his vocal style.

For six months, they posted new videos on YouTube. Justin personally responded to fans who posted comments. He used fans' names and talked with them like long-lost friends. He was approachable. He was accessible. He was handsome and talented. He was everything Braun thought he needed to be – except for one thing.

Record label executives weren't willing to gamble on an unknown teenage singer.

"They kept telling me, 'He's not backed by Disney. He doesn't have a TV show. He's a nobody,'" Braun told *Time*.

While industry executives weren't biting, news of Justin's talent was spreading quickly

told the *New York Times*. "I said, 'Justin? You mean Justin Timberlake?'"

Yes, the six-time Grammy winner was flying Bieber to Los Angeles to talk about possible music deals.

Usher, not wanting to miss out on what could be the next big thing, jumped into action. He was not about to lose a bidding war with Timberlake. Usher could take Bieber shopping. He could rearrange his schedule to meet before the teen flew to California.

Eventually, Usher won out. His prize?

He got to be part of the team that would propel Justin from small-town Canadian unknown to musical superstar. It was a prize he would share with the world.

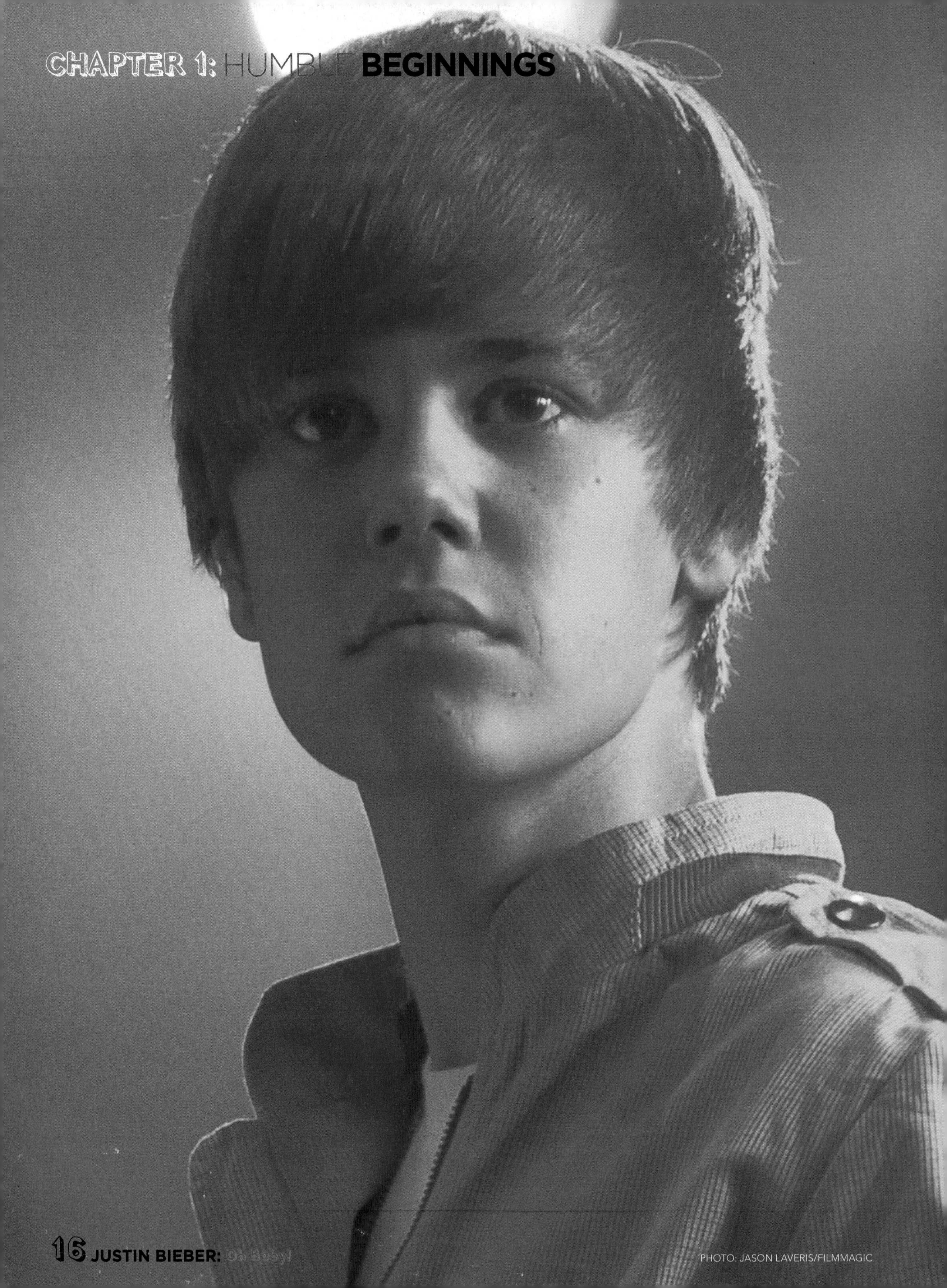

PHOTO: JASON LAVERIS/FILMMAGIC

Justin the Student

No matter how popular he is, Justin Bieber still has to take algebra and biology classes. Sure, he has a private tutor now, but it wasn't long ago that he was a regular kid attending regular school.

Stop by Stratford, Ontario, Canada, and you can check out the three schools where he studied and hung out with friends:

Jeanne Sauvé Catholic School, an elementary French immersion school named after a Canadian journalist, politician and the 23rd Governor General of Canada.

Stratford Northwestern Public School, where approximately 210 students attend classes in seventh and eighth grades. His favorite classes were English with Mr. Monteith and history with Miss Booker.

Stratford Northwestern Secondary School, for grades nine to 12, is the last school Justin attended before relocating to Atlanta. It's one of three high schools in Stratford.

JUSTIN

BIEBER

Chapter 2: Am I Dreaming?

CHAPTER 2:
AM I **DREAMING?**

One day Justin Bieber was a typical teenager in a small Canadian town, hanging out at the skate park with his friends.

The next, he was flying to Atlanta, being introduced to megacelebrities, and wading through life-changing legal contracts with music industry executives.

"My head was definitely spinning," Justin told newscaster Katie Couric on her webcast *@KatieCouric.com*. "I mean, I was like, 'Am I dreaming?' It was a surreal moment."

And those moments just keep coming.

After Justin's famous parking-lot introduction to Usher, the R&B star went to bat for the then-unknown singer.

"When I met him, his personality just won me over," Usher told the *Los Angeles Times*. "And then, when he sang, I realized we were dealing with the real thing. His voice just spoke to the type of music I would want to be associated with. And it wasn't a gimmick – we had to teach him how to dance and be on stage, but he really had a good voice."

Justin and his mom moved to Atlanta in 2007. Pattie gave up her job as a web designer to become full-time mother and

Justin traded in his life of school and hanging out with buddies for tutoring and voice and dance lessons.

Justin Bieber appears on NBC's *Today* television program in New York in October 2009.

Usher and Justin Bieber attend Antonio 'L.A.' Reid's post-Grammy dinner hosted by Jay-Z.

Meanwhile, Braun and Usher went to work building a fan base, developing a plan for Justin's musical career, and recording original music. Ultimately, Usher helped him land a deal and formed a joint-venture label with Scooter Braun and Island Def Jam Music Group's chairman, Antonio "L.A." Reid.

Justin's talent is obvious, but Braun and Usher were quick to assemble a team that would help create a complete, polished package. Road manager and stylist Ryan Good – sometimes referred to as Justin's "swagger coach" – helped put together

JUSTIN'S MUSIC IS COLOR-BLIND

In May 2010 Justin Bieber was nominated by Black Entertainment Television (BET) for an award as Best New Artist of the Year. It was a nomination that raised a lot of eyebrows. Why? Because BET is an American cable network that was started in 1980 with a target audience of young African-American viewers. Much of the music on the network is rap or R&B and most of it is performed by black artists – which Justin is not.

Both MTV and *Rolling Stone* called Justin's nomination the "biggest surprise" of the 2010 BET Awards. Those publications and others pointed out the obvious: Justin's skin is significantly paler than that of other nominees; other contenders in his category were Young Money, Melanie Fiona, Nicki Minaj and Wale.

Music mogul Sean "P. Diddy" Combs came to Justin's defense, telling the *New York Daily News*: "The awards are important to hip-hop and to show (hip-hop artists) in the right light. But the beauty of BET is, if Justin Bieber's hot, then he deserves to be on that stage. Sometimes, at other award shows, the color of your skin or the type of music you make takes away from getting the accolades you deserve."

Stephen Hill, BET's president of music programing and specials, agreed with P. Diddy's assessment, noting that Justin's music has broad appeal.

"Bieber has crossed the color boundaries the same way that hip-hop has crossed the boundaries the other way for a number of years," Hill told Reuters news service. "He also has inspired teen stampedes and regular Twitter trends. He's had rhythm in his music. He makes the type of music our audience likes."

Justin replied to his critics through Twitter: "Thank u to BET for nominating me for Best New Artist @ the BET Awards

Justin and Monica visit BET's 106 & Park at BET Studios on March 22, 2010, in New York City.

this year!! This is an incredible honor and I'm very grateful … read some articles about my bet nomination n i think this goes 2 show that music is color blind … Music is the universal language no matter the country we are born in or the color of our skin. Brings us all together."

Usher and Justin perform during Z100's Jingle Ball at Madison Square Garden in December 2009.

"When he sang, I realized we were dealing with the real thing."

a look that's all his own. Justin is now commonly seen wearing oversized baseball caps, bulky, untied skate shoes, dog tags, and hoodies.

"(Good) has helped me with my style and just putting different pieces together and being able to layer and stuff like that," Bieber told the *Toronto Star*. "(He) helps me and teaches me different swaggerific things

to do."

While Good has worked on style, other staff members have taken on equally important coaching roles. Publicist Melissa Victor has worked with Justin on interview techniques and follows up with reporters whose stories aren't quite as flattering as she'd like. And bodyguard Kenny Hamilton isn't afraid to take Justin aside and scold him if

he finds the singer's behavior to be at all questionable. There is a tutor and hairstylist and makeup artist and scheduler and dozens of other behind-the-scenes folks making sure Justin is wearing what he should and doing what he should, *when* he should.

Mom Pattie – who's like the captain of Team Bieber – says she rests easier knowing her son is surrounded by so many good people.

"(They) protect his character and treat him like a kid, and make sure that he stays grounded and has fun," she said on *The Oprah Winfrey Show,* "I think I would worry more if he was in high school where I wouldn't know what he was doing, whereas now I know who he's with and where he is all the time."

Justin and the rest of the crew's hard work has obviously paid off. His first single, "One Time," was released on July 7, 2009, and reached the Top 20 in five countries.

His first album, "My World," was released in November 2009. It debuted at No. 6 on the Billboard 200. Within a month of release, the album was certi- fied Gold (500,000 sold) in the United States by the Record- ing Industry Associa- tion of America; less than two months later, the album had its U.S. Platinum certification (1 million copies sold).

Four tracks – "One Time," "One Less Lonely Girl," "Favorite Girl" and "Love Me" – were all released before the album and all became hits. That statistic made Justin the first solo artist to have four Top 40 singles before the release of his first album. All seven of the album's songs have

since made it into the Top 40.

While Justin's management team has always had high expectations, others initially doubted how his huge online fan base would translate to the real world. As a result, Justin had a series of fall 2009

Track list

1 One Time
2 Favorite Girl
3 Down to Earth
4 Bigger
5 One Less Lonely Girl
6 First Dance
7 Love Me
8 One Less Lonely Girl [Multimedia]
9 One Time [Multimedia]

appearances at which the host venues were completely unprepared for the crowd that awaited him.

For example, New York radio station WHTZ-FM hosted an online chat with Justin in September 2009.

"When the chat started, it nearly crashed the system and we had record-breaking numbers for any chat we've ever done," WHTZ program director Sharon Datsur told the *National*

Post. "We started playing his music shortly after that."

A few weeks later, more than 2,000 fans showed up for Jus- tin's *Today* show performance. According to NBC network executives, it was the largest crowd assembled to watch any act on the show in 2009.

Then, on November 20, 2009, things got really out of hand when Justin was sched- uled to appear at Long Island's Roosevelt Field Mall. The mall's Justice store was hosting a CD signing and performance that afternoon. By 7 a.m., however, several thousand girls and their parents had arrived at the mall. Not long after that, the crowd became overly aggressive, young children were separated from their parents, injuries

Justin and his mom, Pattie, attend the White House Correspondents' Dinner pre-party in Washington, D.C., on May 1, 2010.

CHAPTER 2: AM I **DREAMING?**

were reported, police were called, and organizers were forced to cancel the event. Authorities told Scooter Braun to send out a Twitter message about the cancellation. The police later charged him with reckless endangerment and criminal nuisance for not sending the message out quickly enough. Police say it took Braun an hour and a half to send two tweets; Braun says it took only seven minutes.

In May 2010, attorneys were still sorting out who was at fault regarding the suburban New York mall event. What isn't up for debate is this: Justin Bieber has more fans – not all of them young girls – than most music industry experts had ever imagined.

Call it Bieber Fever or Biebermania or even Bieber-hysteria. More and more fans are being drawn to this baby-faced, sweet-voiced teen. They wear T-shirts bearing his likeness, hang posters of him in their rooms, and buy his music – both via download and on CD. At a time when much of the rest of the music industry is stagnant – global sales dropped 7.2 percent in 2009 – Justin has created his own personal sales and media tsunami.

And the fervor just continues to build.

When Justin released the second part of his album – *My World 2.0* – in March 2010, it debuted at No. 1 on the

Justin met singer Rihanna at the BET Studios. He brought her flowers; she gave him a kiss on the cheek.

SCOTT "Scooter" BRAUN

Scott "Scooter" Braun's friends and family expected he would become a lawyer and go into politics. He had, after all, been president of his high school class.

As far as Braun's concerned, there's no Senate race or litigating in his near future. He's found success in a very difficult arena: entertainment.

Braun is founder and chief executive officer of Scooter Braun Projects. His achievements have been notable enough to gain him recognition on *Billboard* magazine's 2009 "30 Under 30" list of top industry players under the age of 30.

Braun grew up in a wealthy family in Greenwich, Connecticut. Some of the guys on his basketball team lived in local housing projects and turned Braun onto rap. That's when his love affair with both hip-hop music and culture began.

He started his first business in 2001, when he was a still a freshman at Emory University, promoting parties on Atlanta's club scene. He was recruited to be So So Def's executive director of marketing when he was just 20. In the eight years since, he's shot through the ranks of the hip-hop industry, becoming a promoter, music agent, media marketer and more. He's starred in music videos,

Before he even heard of Justin Bieber, entertainment mogul Scooter Braun, left, had discovered and signed rapper Asher Roth.

negotiated deals, partied with Britney Spears and Ashton Kutcher, and discovered two breakout artists in the past few years.

That's right. Even before he'd laid eyes on Justin Bieber, Braun had signed rapper Asher Roth whose debut album, "Asleep in the Bread Aisle,"

debuted at No. 1 on iTunes and No. 5 on Billboard's Top 200. And just how did he find Roth? On the social networking site MySpace.

Scooter Braun Projects encompasses a wide range of music, television, film and consulting ventures including Schoolboy Records, RBMG, SB Consulting, SB Management and Sheba Publishing.

People who know and have worked with Braun tend to use one word to describe him: "hustla."

"It's not just hustle, it's focused hustle," Ludacris' manager Chaka Zulu told *Atlanta Creative Loafing* newspaper. "He takes the opportunity and knows how to stretch it."

Braun flies his "hustla" flag proudly.

"I think the urban community uses 'hustla' as the ultimate honor," he told *Atlanta Creative Loafing*. "A hustla is somebody who doesn't take no for an answer; somebody who has a vision and a goal and works to realize it; somebody who works his (butt) off to make it happen."

CHAPTER 2: AM I
DREAMING?

Billboard 200 chart, selling 283,000 copies in its first week. Those sales broke a 47-year-old record and made Justin the youngest solo male act to top the Billboard charts since 1963. When the album sold even more copies in its second week, Justin became the first performer since The Beatles to have an album debut at No. 1 and then go on to have even higher sales the following week.

While adult music listeners haven't exactly embraced Justin in the same way tweens and teens have, there's a growing awareness of him and an appreciation for what he's doing.

Even celebrities like singer Sean Kingston (who teamed up with him for the song "Eenie Meenie"), Taylor Swift (he was the opening act for several of her United Kingdom shows), and Rihanna (who gave him a peck on the cheek when they met at an industry party) now count themselves among Justin's many admirers.

"He is amazing," musician Akon told *Hollyscoop.com*. "That kid deserves everything he is getting. He is a hard worker. He always wanted it, since he was seven. He caught the market at the right time. He caught that window right when there were no child stars out there. On top of that he is talent, he is real talent."

No, Justin, this is not a dream.

Justin Bieber onstage at Nickelodeon's 23rd Annual Kids' Choice Awards held at UCLA's Pauley Pavilion on March 27, 2010, in Los Angeles, California.

STARS CHAT ABOUT Justin

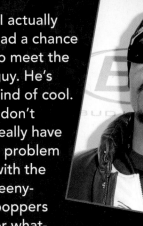

"That guy is a force of nature."
Actor and *Saturday Night Live* head writer Seth Meyers to *People*

"Of course, he's, like, a really cool friend of mine. But he's definitely super talented."
Actor Jasmine Villegas to *MTV News*

"That's my little bro. I'm gonna support him and be excited for him."
Singer Sean Kingston to *MTV News*

"I'm not necessarily a fan. I don't listen to that kind of music."
Singer/actor Miley Cyrus to *MTV*

"Having this type of success at this age can be very over-whelming. I'm really happy that I'm able to pull from my own experiences to help him understand how to handle it."
Singer/actor Usher to *Good Morning America*

"Oh, man! Bieber Fever, man, call the doctor. I got it bad!"
- Actress Victoria Justice to *MTV News*

"I love me some Justin Bieber. What a great guy. He's such a talented guy ... 16 he's going through right now. ... That dude started as a YouTube sensation ... Now he's selling out and people are rioting in Australia? What's going on? That's amazing and so cool that the Internet is so powerful you can do stuff like that."
Talk show host Jimmy Fallon on *Late Night With Jimmy Fallon*

"I actually had a chance to meet the guy. He's kind of cool. I don't really have a problem with the teeny-boppers or what-not. Once upon a time, I was a young teenager coming into the game, driving 'em crazy ... I wish him luck and success ..."
Rapper Snoop Dogg to *MTV*

"He's a cutie-pie!"
Singer Rihanna to *E! Online*

"What you see on TV and in all the YouTube videos is really what you get in real life. He's a really nice guy. You can tell that what he's got comes from his hard work ethic."
Actor Mathias Anderle to *JustSoYouKnow.com*

"I don't get this Bieber thing. I really don't get it ... I haven't even heard his music. I couldn't tell you one name of his songs – and I'm not lying about that."
Singer/actor Matthew Morrison on *E! Online*

"Oh, man!
Bieber Fever, man,
call the doctor.
I got it bad!"

Victoria Justice, *MTV News*

Family Guy

Justin Bieber's dad, Jeremy, split with his mom back when Justin was just two years old. Justin has since become a big brother – twice. Dad Jeremy and his new wife, Erin Wagner Bieber, live in Winnipeg, Manitoba, Canada. Justin's half-sister, Jazmyn Bieber, was born in May 2008; his half-brother, Jaxson Bieber, was born in November 2009. Justin tweeted about Jaxon's birth: "Best Week Ever = Releasing your first album and having your baby bro born the same week. Awesome"

Justin says family is a priority for him. He generally travels with his mom. When she can't make it, dad sometimes fills in.

Justin even took time out of his super busy schedule to help Jazmyn celebrate her birthday. His May 30, 2010, tweets document the event:

"Today is my lil sis' bday .. told everyone I couldn't make it … then put on my disguise and SURPRISE!! Ha Ha SURPRISE JAZZY – I couldn't let you celebrate 2 alone … even surprised my Jaxon. LOL."

JUSTIN

BIEBER

Chapter 3: The Snowball Effect

CHAPTER 3:
THE SNOWBALL EFFECT

Take a baseball-sized snowball and roll it down the side of a hill. As it goes, it gathers more snow and whatever else is in its path: rocks, twigs, leaves. The bigger the snowball gets, the faster it goes. It's called the snowball effect.

Justin Bieber's career has been a lot like that — his fame has grown more quickly than most who have gone before him.

Everywhere he goes — from the concert stage to the red carpet to lunch at an out-of-the-way restaurant — his high energy and boyish charm trigger explosions of camera flashes. Over one weekend in December 2009, he performed at Madison Square Garden, taped a performance for *Dick Clark's New Year's Rockin' Eve with Ryan Seacrest*, and then sand "Someday at Christmas" for President and Mrs. Obama at the White House.

By the time Justin released "My World" in November 2009, he had 50 million YouTube subscribers and was one of the most discussed topics on Twitter. By April 2010, he had more

Justin's schedule is packed with talk show appearances, CD signings, and performances such as one for *Dick Clark's New Year's Rockin' Eve with Ryan Seacrest*. (RIGHT) Justin sings with Selena Gomez.

" By the time Justin released *My World* in November 2009 he had 50 million YouTube subscribers..."

JUSTIN BIEBER: *Oh Baby!* **37**

Justin's fans long for a touch at this February 2010 performance in Miami Beach, Florida.

than 2.5 million Facebook fans, 1.7 million Twitter followers, and 2.5 million MySpace fans.

Despite his megastar status, Justin replies to fans when he can.

"I still (use Twitter) as much as before," he told the *National* *Post*. "People write to me and say, 'I'm giving up, you're not talking to me.' I just write them a simple message like, 'Never give up,' you know? And it changes their life."

And the snowball keeps rolling.

Justin joined Taylor Swift for several shows on the United Kingdom leg of her tour. In April 2010 he was the musical guest star on *Saturday Night Live* and got rave reviews for an awkward teacher-student comedy sketch

MUSICAL INSPIRATIONS

These days, it's Justin Bieber who is inspiring young kids to pick up the guitar or sing along with their favorite artists. But it wasn't that long ago that he was looking for inspiration from musicians who had gone before him.

"I grew up listening to a lot of older stuff, like Boyz II Men and Stevie Wonder and Michael Jackson," he told *MojoTV.com*. "I actually took it real hard when Michael Jackson passed. He was an inspiration to so many people, including Usher, but his legend lives on. I just love his music, along with just old soul music. It's just awesome."

So, which other artists inspire Justin?

His mentor, Usher, certainly makes the list, as do Justin Timberlake, Lil Wayne, Ludacris, Jay Shawn, Corrine Bailey, B.O.B., and The

Justin and Ryan Seacrest prepare to watch 'Captain EO' with more than 500 fans at Disneyland in March 2010.

Dream. He's also a big fan of Travis Barker, the drummer who gained fame playing with Blink-182 and The Transplants.

"I definitely had people that I looked up to," he told *MacLeans* magazine. "But he advises aspiring young artists to be themselves and be

original – not carbon copies of someone else.

"I looked up to Michael Jackson and Stevie Wonder and Boyz II Men," he says. "But I never tried to sound like anybody."

Justin performs onstage at the 2010 Nickelodeon Upfront Presentation at Hammerstein Ballroom on March 11, 2010, in New York City.

he performed with actress Tina Fey. In May he appeared with his mom on *The Oprah Winfrey Show* and threw out the ceremonial first pitch at the Chicago White Sox's U.S. Cellular Field. His baby face has been featured on magazine covers including *People, J-14, Twist, Billboard* and *Bop.*

His fame has grown more quickly than most who have gone before him.

On April 26, 2010, Justin had to cancel a free show in Sydney, Australia, after a crowd of about 5,000 fans got rowdy. The pushing and shoving resulted in minor injuries to eight fans; two others fainted.

Justin later ended up singing one song live on local TV and apologized to those who had waited to see him perform at his only Australian gig.

"I am so sorry that it got out of control, we don't want anyone to get hurt. It gets crazy sometimes," he said.

Two days later, fans went nuts again, this time mobbing Justin at the airport in Auckland, New Zealand. He used Twitter to

PHOTO: BRYAN BEDDER/GETTY IMAGES

reach out to his nearly 2 million followers: "Finally got to New Zealand last night. The airport was crazy. Not happy that some- one stole my hat and knocked down my mama. Come on people …"

Justin's fans have even caused an online riot of sorts.

"Ladies calm down," he tweeted after discovering

Kim Kardashian, whom he met at the White House Cor- respondents' dinner, had been receiving death threats from

Now, it's Justin Bieber's turn.

fans who were unhappy about their new friendship.

Justin quickly went to work assuring fans that the *Keeping*

Up with the Kardashians star was not his girlfriend. He tweeted that Kim is "a very sexy friend but a friend. No need 4 threats. Let's all be friends and hang out often."

Despite causing riots on both sides of the equator and in the real and virtual worlds, the teen heartthrob fearlessly goes about his music-making. His

THE HAIR

Sure fans adore Justin's talent, but well, his hair has its own admirers.

Justin isn't the only teen boy to wear long side-swept bangs, but he's able to flick and flip it out of his eyes with a style that's all his own. Many fans agree the allure is in the flipping.

A video of Justin blow- drying his hair was posted on YouTube as a promotion for his MTV special, *The Diary of Justin Bieber*. Thousands have tuned in just to watch him towel-dry his light brown locks and then dry it all forward.

Justin says he doesn't spend much time on his mop top.

"I just get out of the shower," he told Radio Disney. "I blow-dry it and then it's done in like five minutes.

Justin told *US Magazine* that he may switch up his famous hairdo – someday.

"I'm kinda liking the long hair right now," he said. "In the future, I may get bored and change it up. But for now I like it how it is."

Talk show host Ellen DeGe- neres wanted to find out how attached the teen idol is to his trademark tresses. When he

appeared on her show in May 2010, she whipped out a pair of scissors in an attempt to snip off a lock or two. No worries. Justin avoided the impromptu haircut.

The New York Times reported in May 2010 that teenage boys were paying as much as $150 to get a 'do like Justin's. One Manhattan stylist said more than half his teen, male clients ask for the shaggy bowl cut.

In a video posted on You- Tube, *ClevverTV*'s Joslyn Davis suggested the popular hair- style, which is often referred to as "the Bieber," deserves a name all its own. Her sugges- tions: the Bieb-alicious or the Bieb-bob.

first headlining tour, featuring Sean Kingston as special guest, opened June 23, 2010, at the 16,000-seat XL Center in Hartford, Connecticut. His My World Tour was scheduled to zigzag across the country, visiting more than 40 cities before wrapping up in Allentown, Penn., on Sept. 4.

He may seem to have come from nowhere, but fans know he's been building his online presence since 2008.

"He was growing slowly and the fans saw that – they felt like they were playing a role in building him to become a star," *Billboard* magazine associate editor Monica Herrera told CNN. "They became invested in championing him,

to keep him in the limelight."

Thirteen-year-old Alicia Isaacson explained Justin's allure to *Time* magazine after seeing him in a private New York City concert.

"He's so sweet," she said.

Union-Tribune. "Then, of course, he has a cute face, nice hair, dresses very stylish and has a nice dimple that only makes him cuter! I love his music! The words, the rhythm and the fact

"He's not like every other guy who is just like, 'Ugh, whatever'."

"He's not like every other guy who is just like, 'Ugh, whatever."

Hannah Montie, an 11-year-old from suburban Buffalo, New York, told the *Buffalo News:*

that he seems to be singing from personal experiences in some of his songs."

There is undoubtedly a special place in American pop culture for the teen idol. For years, young girls have fallen hopelessly in love with musicians. Elvis Presley, The Beatles, Donny Osmond, David Cassidy, Shaun Cassidy, Leif Garrett, Justin Timberlake and The Jonas Brothers have all been teen heartthrobs. They've adorned magazine covers, sold out concerts, signed countless autographs and had their faces plastered on T-shirts and posters.

Now, it's Justin Bieber's turn to take on that role. And, despite the lack of privacy, it's a part he's happy to play.

"I think I'm in the right business," he told *MacLeans* magazine. "I've always loved to be the center of attention."

And the snowball keeps on rolling.

IN APRIL 2010 JUSTIN WAS THE MUSICAL GUEST ON SATURDAY NIGHT LIVE AND GOT RAVE REVIEWS FOR AN AWKWARD TEACHER-STUDENT COMEDY SKETCH HE PERFORMED WITH ACTRESS TINA FEY.

whether it was buying his albums or watching his videos or tweeting about him, they all had a stake in wanting

"He's definitely really cute and he has an amazing voice."

"He is hot, very hot," California 12-year-old Daniella Corrales told the *San Diego*

Reality TV star Kim Kardashian and Justin attend the 2010 White House Correspondents' dinner pre-party in Washington, D.C.

Tweet Treat

Justin Bieber has more than 2 million fans on Twitter, making him one of the most-followed people on the service.

His manager, Scooter Braun, told attendees at a worldwide Internet conference called TechCrunch Disrupt 2010 that, for the most part, Justin is actually the one doing the tweeting. Braun says he's the only other person with the password to the account and when he tweets,

it's clear the messages are coming from him – not Justin.

"The usage of Twitter is important," said Braun, "because it shows that the same person who was talking to (fans) before he got huge is still talking to them now."

Some days Justin sends out more than 20 messages via the service. Here's a random sampling of his tweets:

➡ Traveling the world and seeing all these places is wild 4 me. Growing up I would never even imagine it possible. Very grateful 2 u 4 this.
9:48 A.M., MAY 18, 2010

➡ Just got to say that Oprah is real nice down to earth person. She even came back after the show to talk with everyone. She is incredible.
1:34 P.M., MAY 4, 2010

➡ In DC running around. We are all getting suited up in tuxes 2nite for the dinner at the White House. Excited to see who is going to be there.
12:47 P.M. MAY 1, 2010

➡ Will never forget 2nite. It was INCREDIBLE!! Thank u for the opportunity and thanks to everyone at SNL and Tina Fey for just being fun.
11:03 P.M., APRIL 10, 2010

➡ Took a nap and then went and hooped.
6:21 P.M., APRIL 5, 2010

➡ Video shoot...school.... video shoot...long day. with good people so all good.
4:33 P.M., MARCH 29, 2010

➡ 3 yrs ago I started a Youtube page in my lil town of 30k people. Now I have my 2nd album coming out and I am living my dream. WHY?? THE FANS.
8:40 P.M., MARCH 26, 2010

➡ LESS than 10 MINUTES to MY WORLD 2.0!! I cannot believe it's here.
7:52 P.M., MARCH 22, 2010

➡ Alot of u have asked what I want for my bday. One thing is BABY at #1
4:55 P.M., FEBRUARY 25, 2010

➡ Girls of London...please don't bang on the windows of the car when we're moving. u can get hurt. no need for that. I got love for all of u :)
4:22 A.M., MARCH 18, 2010

➡ Great night. Went to Six Flags and hit the rides and played some bball. I told you guys ... still a normal kid. Good times had by all.
11:56 P.M., FEBRUARY 15, 2010

➡ Got with my new band today... killer. Excited for touring. Drummer is nuts.
7:02 P.M., JANUARY 25, 2010

➡ Long day running around London having fun. The UK has a lot of music shows on tv.
2:06 P.M., JANUARY 15, 2010

Justin plays for fans during his visit to the Nintendo World store in New York City.

JUSTIN BIEBER: Oh Baby! **47**

Justin belts out a tune at the 2010 White House Easter Egg Roll. The event, held on the South Lawn of the White House, was hosted by President Obama.

"I looked up to Michael Jackson and Stevie Wonder and Boyz II Men, but I never tried to sound like anybody."

CHAPTER 3: THE **SNOWBALL EFFECT**

Face-Off

Justin Bieber's opening pitch at the May 3, 2010, Chicago White Sox game was about four feet wide of the strike zone. "I need to work on my curveball," he tweeted that night. "Hey, I'm Canadian. We play hockey ..."

That's right. Justin feels much more at home on the ice than the pitcher's mound. In fact, he's been playing hockey pretty much since he could walk.

"I love hockey," he told *ABC News*. "I've played hockey all my life."

Justin, himself, is a center forward, but his touring schedule doesn't allow for much ice time these days.

Instead, he finds himself cheering on his favorite teams. He was ecstatic when Canada won the gold in both men's and women's ice hockey at the 2010 Olympics in Vancouver.

He also likes to get to games when he can to cheer on his hometown team, the Toronto Maple Leafs.

"I'm a Leafs fan, yeah," he said.

Forget hardball – certainly Justin's fans would like to see him on skates!

JUSTIN

BIEBER

Chapter 4: Still a Kid at Heart

CHAPTER 4:
STILL A
KID AT HEART

Justin Bieber has been thrown into the very adult business world. He has lawyers and accountants and schedulers. He sits through meetings. He helps make hiring decisions.

But, no matter how "adult" he's sometimes forced to be, Justin is still a kid at heart.

This is a guy who still likes to skateboard down hallways and play video games just before he goes on stage. And he doesn't always listen to his mother.

bodyguard, Kenny Hamilton: "Justin needs to stop or he's losing that phone. He won't listen to me! Don't let him on the elevator, Kenny, unless he gets off that phone."

Justin didn't get off the phone, the doors of the elevator closed, and mom, son and bodyguard were left to finish their squabble in privacy.

Later, in the hotel lobby, Justin's mom told the *Times* reporter: "No 15-year-old wants to be around his mother 24/7. And no mother wants to be around her

> No matter how "adult" he's sometimes forced to be, Justin is still a **kid at heart.**

When a *New York Times* reporter hung out with him and his handlers in preparation for a feature story, the reporter noted he jumped out of the van ahead of the rest of the group and raced through the hotel lobby. His mother, Pattie Mallette, chased after him, shouting orders to both Justin and his

15-year-old 24/7, either."

As frustrated as she may become with her son, Mallette understands that Justin's sometimes annoying teenage behavior is just about the only "regular" thing about him. Photographers camp outside his hotel room, waiting to snap his image; any mistake or

PHOTO: NOEL VASQUEZ/GETTY IMAGES

Fans wait outside for the Justin Bieber concert at the Hollywood Palladium.

awkward moment is recorded on video and posted online almost instantly. Every single thing he does – whether he's having lunch with a friend or walking headfirst into a glass door – is reported on entertainment gossip websites.

That's why Justin's mom and management team do whatever they can to bring normalcy to his very extraordinary routine.

"We try to take off at least one

> **"(If I misbehave) my mom takes things away that I really like, like my computer, my phone."**

day a week for me to be a regular kid, go play basketball, hang out with my friends and, you know, just do what I like to do," Justin said on *The Oprah Winfrey Show*. "Sometimes for that day I just

sleep all day because the six days before I'm exhausted."

And just because he's a superstar doesn't mean he's going to get by with breaking curfew, losing his temper, or

ABOUT THAT TATTOO

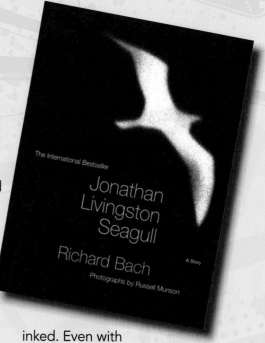

The blogosphere went into overdrive in May 2010. That's when it was revealed that Justin Bieber had gotten a tattoo several months earlier, for his sixteenth birthday.

Brian Byrne, co-owner of Toronto's Son of a Gun Tattoo and Barbershop where Justin got inked, said the pop star came to his shop with his dad, Jeremy. Justin got a very small Jonathan Livingston Seagull tattoo on his lower, left abdomen. *Jonathan Livingston Seagull* is a book from the early 1970s written by Richard Bach; it's a novella about the importance of seeking high purpose in life, even if others are threatened by your ambition.

"From what I can gather, I guess a bunch of people in his family actually have that same tattoo, his dad included," Byrne told *MTV News*.

Getting body art is not without pain, but Byrne said Justin didn't shed a tear.

"He was a super nice kid," Byrne said. "He was nice in our shop, he didn't cry or anything like that. It went really well. It was really cool to have him here."

Canada has no age restrictions for those getting tattoos, but some shops – including the one Justin visited – require minors to have their parents' permission before getting

inked. Even with parental consent, Son of a Gun reserves the right to refuse to tattoo distasteful designs. Byrne said he had no problems with Justin's request because it was a family tradition.

Justin performs at the Pepsi
Super Bowl Fan Jam in Miami
Beach, Florida.

refusing to follow rules.

"(If I misbehave) my mom takes things away that I really like, like my computer, my phone," he told Winfrey. "She takes my phone away for a couple of days and I'm like, 'Oh, I need that!'"

Obviously surprised that his mom is such a strict disciplinarian, Winfrey asked: "You can't say, 'Mom, I can't get grounded – I'm Justin Bieber?'"

Justin replied: "She'd slap me in the face!"

Fortunately, Mallette's strategy of treating her son like any other kid seems to be working. Despite his megafame, he's a surprisingly normal teen who enjoys bowling, skateboarding and golfing.

Justin gets to fly his best buds from Canada to see him every month or so.

For his 16th birthday – on March 1, 2010 – Justin invited friends to an extravagant party in Los Angeles, where he and his guests played paintball, basketball, laser tag and sumo-wrestled. When he was in New Zealand in spring 2010, he decided to spend his day off jumping off a bridge – bungee jumping, that is. And, in Australia, he and his buddies used their downtime to hit the beach and toss around a football.

"I'm only 16 once," he told the *National Post*. "I've got to live like it."

And then, of course, there are girls.

Justin has flirted with celebri-

Ten Totally Random Facts About Justin

1. His favorite color is purple.

2. He got a Range Rover from Usher for his 16th birthday.

3. His favorite food is Spaghetti Bolognese.

4. Boyz II Men's *II* is his favorite album of all time.

5. He loves candy – especially Sour Patch Kids.

6. English is his favorite subject in school.

7. Chuck Norris is one of Justin's heroes. He frequently mentions the actor in his tweets.

8. Justin is left-handed.

9. He's looking for a girl with a good sense of humor and a nice smile.

10. Even though he's known for his hair, he's not devoted to any specific brand of shampoo. Rather, he says he uses whatever is in the hotel.

Justin poses on the Red Carpet at the 2010 Juno Awards in Saint John's, Canada.

ties ranging from Beyonce and Selena Gomez to First Lady Michelle Obama and veteran (as in 55 years older than him!) journalist Barbara Walters.

When he flirted with comedian Chelsea Handler on her talk show *Chelsea Lately,* she warned the teen idol: "Please just keep yourself together because sooner or later you're going be Justin Timberlake … and then you can't flirt around anymore because then you're going to have to follow up on your flirting and you're really going have to close some deals. So, be careful what you wish for, little nugget."

Justin says he has received lots of marriage proposals from crazed fans. Even though he doesn't plan on getting married anytime soon, he doesn't rule out the idea of someday dating a fan.

"It depends on what the situation is," he told *People* magazine. "I think that I'm not going to limit myself."

JUSTIN'S SUPER FANS

In September 2009, Canadian teenager Tricia Maltibag won a shout out from Justin at the MTV Video Music Awards. In her video entry, she claimed she was Justin's biggest fan, having listened to "One Time" more than 1,000 times.

"My friends think I'm a little bit obsessed," she said in her video. "But I'm not. I'm just being a true fan because you are such an inspiration."

MTV News talked with her after her win and she expressed excitement over being recognized by the pop star for her devotion to him.

Since Maltibag won the *VMA*-sponsored contest, Justin has released two albums and his popularity has soared. But she says she's okay with the fact that his army of followers has swelled.

"As for me, I'm pretty much his biggest fan, though some might disagree – but my room looks like Bieber Fever has exploded all over the walls … my friends are pretty shocked when they come in and I can't stop talking about him and a quarter of my wardrobe is Bieber attire," she told *MTV News.* Shortly after the *VMAs,* Maltibag went to Montreal with friends and waited in line 12 hours to meet her pop idol.

"I always knew he would make it big — I just didn't know it would be this fast. I'm so proud, but I still miss the days when he was a small-town boy who did notice girls like me," she continued. "But I support him 110 percent and I'm so glad that his name is really out there, so he can finally share his talent with the world, as corny as that sounds."

Of course, not all Justin's fans – or SUPER fans – are teens and tweens. Take for example, the three-year-old Oregon girl named Cody whose YouTube video of her crying and proclaiming her love for Justin went viral. The nearly five-minute video collected more than 10

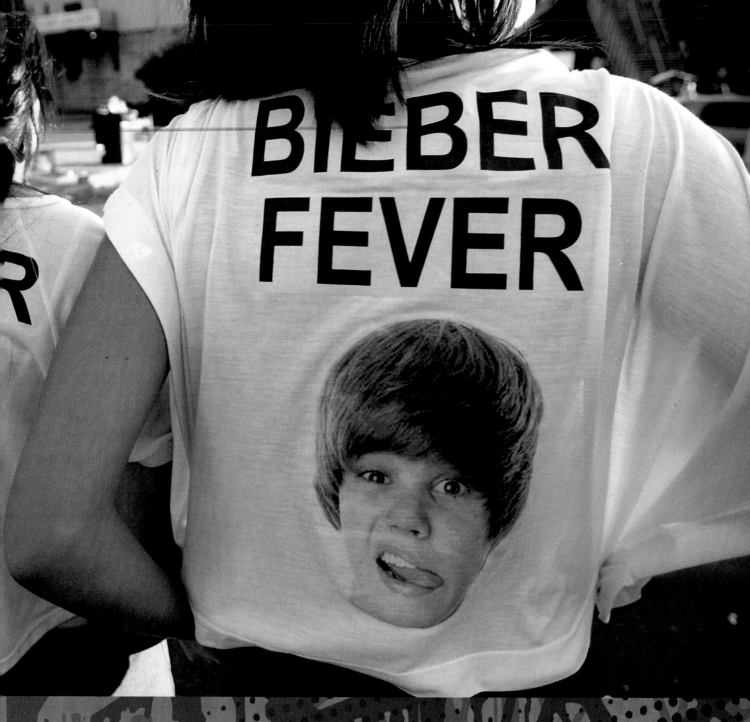

million views in its first four months after it was posted.

Asked in her video why she loves Justin Bieber, the sobbing girl says: "Because I know he loves me back." She says she's sad because she doesn't "get to see Justin Bieber all day."

Talk show host Jimmy Kimmel brought the young girl and pop star together on his show, *Jimmy Kimmel Live!*, in March 2010. Cody was practically

speechless when Justin was introduced to her backstage. Her tears wiped away – at least for the moment – the girl hugged Justin tight and announced she would like to marry him.

Another of Justin's super fans is, surprisingly 34 years old. And male.

Mick Follers describes himself as Justin's No. 1 fan and he has the license plates to prove it. That's right, the forklift operator

from Sydney, Australia, has paid $440 a year for the privilege of having personalized plates for his car.

Follers has never seen Justin perform live, but he's faithfully followed his career on Twitter, YouTube and Facebook.

"I've downloaded all his tunes from iTunes," he told the *Daily Telegraph*.

"I'm one of his older fans, but I like his stuff."

The teen heartthrob told the *Associated Press* in May 2010 that he doesn't have a girlfriend and is just "hanging out" with a few girls. His hectic travel schedule, he said, doesn't allow him to get too serious in his relationships.

When he does go out with a girl, they're likely to head to a movie and maybe grab a bite to eat – all as discreetly as possible and under the watchful eye of his body guard. More public dates are simply out of the question considering the riots Justin seems to cause wherever he goes.

"I definitely miss being able to walk around the mall and

"I think I'm still immature sometimes, but I try not to think I'm **hot stuff.**"

stuff, but I love what I am doing and I love that I can perform for millions of people and have their support," he told *Time* magazine. "But there are ups and downs, you know, like everything else."

The "ups" Justin talks about are obvious. His music is being heard around the world, he's landing gigs that many veteran performers can't land, and he's raking in some serious cash. The "downs" for Justin come in the

form of losing his privacy and missing out some of the things normal teenagers experience.

"I am with adults all day and it's fun," he told the *Los Angeles Times*. "Sometimes, I'm like, 'No, I want to hang out with my friends my own age.' But at the same time, it makes me mature a little faster. I think I'm still immature sometimes, but I try not to think I'm hot stuff."

Justin's charm appeals to ladies young and old. Here, he serenades an obviously happy fan.

Fans cheer as Justin performs a free concert in Los Angeles' Nokia Plaza.

NOT **EVERYONE** LOVES JUSTIN

Justin Bieber's fans love him because he's wholesome and flirty. They adore his boyish good looks and in-his-eyes bangs. They swoon when he sings and shows off his dance moves.

Justin's anti-fans hate him for the very same reasons.

They say he's too wholesome, too short, too flirty. They make jokes about his hair and they criticize his voice. They've formed Facebook pages for "Non-Beliebers" and have created websites that question whether he's really a boy.

What drives the hate is unclear. Perhaps jealousy or differing musical tastes are to blame. Regardless of the reason for their rants, Justin haters are a vocal group.

So, how does a teenager handle all that hate?

For the most part, Justin simply tries to laugh off the nasty comments. Deep down, he knows his real fans and friends are what really matter.

"There's more people that like me than there are who hate me, so I kind of brush it off," he told the *National Post*. "People say, 'Oh, people just like him because he's pretty.' Or, the funniest one: 'When he goes through puberty, he's not going to be a good singer anymore.' How does that make sense when we've seen people like Michael Jackson and Usher and Justin Timberlake do it?"

"I definitely miss being able to walk around the mall and stuff, but I love what I am doing and I love that I can perform for millions of people and have their support."

Justin visits New York's Nintendo
World store in September 2009.

First Fan Foul-Up

Oops … Justin Bieber says the first time he performed at the White House, as part of a 2009 holiday performance, President Barack Obama mispronounced his name. (The president called him "Justin BYE-ber.")

It's a blunder Justin is more than willing to forgive.

"He messed up my name, but I give it to him. He's not (the) age category I sing to. He's not 'One Less Lonely Girl,'" Justin told People magazine.

While Justin is Canadian, he's honored to have also performed at the 2010 White House Easter Egg Roll and to have attended the White House Correspondents' Dinner.

"It was great," Justin told MTV News. "(Obama) was really cool, really nice and I was happy to be there."

Reportedly, Obama's daughters, Sasha and Malia, are big Bieber fans. "We met them, took pictures with them, took pictures with the First Lady."

PHOTO: ASSOCIATED PRESS

JUSTIN

BIEBER

Chapter 5: Beyond the Here & Now

CHAPTER 5:
BEYOND THE
HERE & NOW

Justin Bieber knew he had hit the big-time back in February 2010, when he walked into a Los Angeles studio to join a platoon of more than 75 celebrities who were recording a "We Are the World" remake to benefit Haiti.

"That was amazing. 'We Are the World'

was incredible," he told *MTV News.* "I got to work with Quincy Jones and Lionel Richie and all the greats … Kanye was there, Lil Wayne … everybody … It was really incredible and I had a great time. It was crazy. Barbra Streisand was on this side of me and Celine

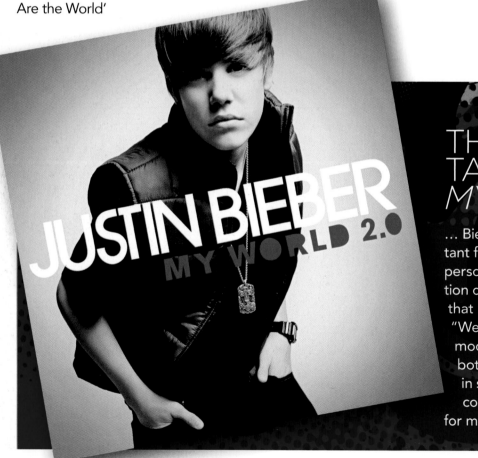

THE CRITICS TALK ABOUT *MY WORLD 2.0*

… Bieber has something more important for a young pop star than chops: personality. He's got an odd combination of guilelessness and swagger that makes puppy-love goop like "We'll take it to the sky/Past the moon/Through the galaxies" sound both sweet and playful. For parents in search of a fresh-faced male counterpart to Taylor Swift — and for millions of tweens looking for a

cute boy who knows his way around a beat — help has arrived. As for the haters? Quoth the Bieber Twitter feed, "I wish u guys the best of luck in ur hating."

Jody Rosen,
Rolling Stone

If we truly want the best for America's children, let us pause and give thanks for Justin Bieber.

After years of humdrum bubblegum from Miley Cyrus and the brothers Jonas, the 16-year-old has thrown a candy-coated wrench into Disney's heartthrob assembly line by giving young fans something worth screaming their lungs out for: lovable pop songs.

Chris Richards,
Washington Post

Bieber's voice is still high, clear, and sweet; when it cracks, that may be a day of reckoning. But there's real talent, it seems, under all that hair.

Leah Greenblatt,
Entertainment Weekly

Aside from being this year's non-threatening pop pretty boy with a silly hairstyle, does Bieber have anything to offer musically? In a word: No. Sure, the Stratford teen seems able to carry a tune. But this undercooked batch of cookie-cutter pop fluff, blue-eyed R&B and first-waltz ballads suggests his world is a pretty one-dimensional place. Hope you're saving your money, kid.

Darryl Sterdan,
Toronto Sun

Musicians Wyclef Jean, Akon, Sean "P. Diddy" Combs, Justin, Sean Kingston (back row), Chris Brown and Robin Thicke perform in BET's SOS Saving Ourselves: Help for Haiti benefit concert and telethon in February 2010 in Miami.

Dion was on the other side of me and I felt like, *This is so big.*"

Justin not only participated in remaking the 25-year-old song, he sang the first verse of "We Are the World" as a solo.

And as "incredible" as it was to meet and perform with so many superstars, the real thrill came at knowing he was helping raise money to support Haiti earthquake relief.

Justin is quickly making a name for himself in the world of philanthropy.

Justin is quickly making a name for himself in the world of philanthropy. He has participated in and supported numerous charitable efforts including:

➡ *Idol Gives Back*, a special broadcast of *American Idol* in which Justin performed alongside Annie Lennox, Mary J. Blige, Elton John and others. The two-hour Fox program raised more than $45 million for Children's Health Fund, Feeding America, Malaria No More, Save the Children's U.S. programs, and the United Nations Foundation.

➡ The Clinton Global Initiative event, a nonpartisan

effort established by the William J. Clinton Foundation to address major global problems.

➯ A joint campaign by the Ricky Martin Foundation and Habitat for Humanity to help victims of the Haiti earthquake.

➯ *Canada for Haiti Telethon*, performing with celebrities including Celine Dion, Avril Lavigne, Drake, and Nelly Furtado.

➯ *SOS Saving Ourselves: Help for Haiti* telethon on BET,

> ## "I got to work with Quincy Jones and Lionel Richie and all the greats ... Kanye was there, Lil Wayne ... everybody."

for which he both answered telephones and performed a medley of his hits.

➯ Women & Children's Hospital of

Buffalo fundraiser in which he performed a private concert for students of the school that raised the most money in

JUSTIN + ? = music

Justin Bieber collaborated with Ludacris on his megahit "Baby."

He teamed up with Sean Kingston on his song "Eenie Meenie."

Usher and Justin partnered on a remake of Usher's song "Somebody to Love." Fellow Canadian Drake joined forces for a "Baby" remix at the 2010 Juno Awards and he's recorded a single called "Rich Girl" with Soulja Boy for an upcoming Dr. Dre album.

Sure, Justin may be one of the hottest solo acts on the planet, but that hasn't stopped him from working with some really talented artists along the way.

So, who else does young Mr. Bieber want to sing with?

"I want to work with Lil Wayne ... once he gets out of jail," he told *E! News* in February 2010.

Other possible future collaborators for Justin? He told the UK press he'd love to record with Taylor Swift: "She's a great writer, songwriter, musician, singer, so she's an all-round great person. I think it would be great."

Rumors have also circulated about possible collaborations with Miley

Justin performs at a Haiti benefit with Sean "P. Diddy" Combs and Sean Kingston.

Cyrus, Filipino singer Charice, and Sean Fox Zastoupil.

Looks like Justin doesn't have to worry about not having a singing partner when he wants one ...

Ludacris and Justin perform together in February 2010 at BET's *SOS Saving Ourselves: Help for Haiti* benefit concert.

JUSTIN BIEBER:

support of the hospital.

Justin also has an ongoing relationship with Pencils of Promise, an organization that helps build schools in developing countries. In October 2009, he participated in a music festival hosted by Free the Children, a charity that empowers children in North America to take action to improve the lives

you are, so he's also determined to keep recording and selling records.

He told *MacLeans* magazine he has great hopes for continuing to grow as an artist. "I just want to excel musically, instrumentation-wise, as well as just my tone in general," he said.

Justin acknowledges that transitioning from teen heart-

"I just want to excel musically, instrumentation-wise, as well as just my tone in general,"

of children overseas.

Justin told a PopDirt.com reporter at that event that he places great importance on giving back.

"The cause is great, helping build schools and such … I just think this whole organization is amazing." Justin added that being involved in charity is "very cool" and noted that girls involved with charities are "definitely" more attractive to him.

As he looks to the future, this rookie pop star promises giving back will remain one of his top priorities. In fact, he hopes to establish his own charitable foundation by the time he turns 17.

And, while he's dedicated to helping others, he knows it's hard to lend your name to projects if no one knows who

throb to adult star won't be easy, but he's up for the challenge. He's hopeful his career will be long, productive and varied.

"I think that as my audience grows with me, that my lyrics will change and they'll be more directed for the older audience," he told *MacLeans*. "I mean, right now I'm singing to young and old. I'm singing to basically anybody who wants to listen."

And he's not afraid to take on critics who wonder what will happen to his vocal range as he goes through puberty.

"I'm at that age where my voice is changing," he told *ABC News* in March 2010. "It's been a pretty smooth transition so far. I'm not all the way through it, but I have the best vocal coaches training me and stuff … I like how it is right now, but I have

Justin sits backstage before performing in North Tonawanda, New York, in April 2010, as part of a contest to benefit Women & Children's Hospital of Buffalo.

to work on it and it's going to get lower, so I have to work with what I have."

Whatever happens in the future, Justin is prepared to work hard. Most immediately, he plans to take a short break after his 2010 North American tour and then head to the studio to produce another album. He knows that some artists toil a lifetime and never achieve the kind of fame he's already known. He knows success can be fleeting and fans can be fickle, but he's grateful for what has already happened.

Girls involved with charities are "definitely" more attractive.

"I feel like I just won the lotto," he told *Time* magazine.

Usher, who will continue to help guide Justin's new career, says he couldn't be more proud of his protégé.

"It's almost like he'd already mapped out in his mind what his story could be, and it's up to us to navigate him," Usher told the *Los Angeles Times*. "There couldn't be anybody more proud. He's like a son to me. And never too much — because this is only the beginning. His story has yet to truly unfold."

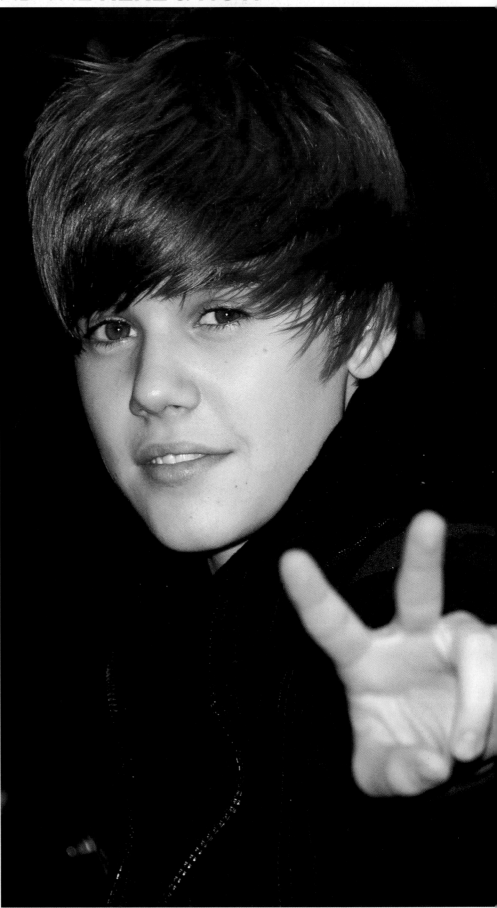

Justin leaves a taping of The *Late Show with David Letterman* in New York. PHOTO: ASSOCIATED PRESS

DEFENDING A FRIEND

When Justin Bieber first found out that he'd be a presenter at the 2009 MTV Video Music Awards (VMAs) he was super excited. Little did he know he'd find himself near the center of the evening's biggest controversy, defending one of his pals.

Singer Taylor Swift was in the middle of her acceptance speech for Best Female Video for her song "You Belong With Me," when rapper Kanye West walked onto the stage.

"I always dreamed about what it would be like to win one of these one day," Taylor said to the crowd. As she continued her speech, West walked up to the microphone and interrupted, saying he thought Beyonce's "Single Ladies" video should have won the award instead.

"Hey, Taylor, I'm really happy for you, but Beyonce had one of the best videos of all time," West told the awards show audience. It

was an awkward moment felt around the world.

When Justin and Mirada Cosgrove took the stage

shortly after that to present an award, Justin took a moment to vocalize his support for his friend, saying: "Give it up for Taylor Swift. She deserved that award." In an interview with the *Vancouver Sun*, Justin said Taylor met him backstage that night to say, "Thanks for sticking up for me, lil' bro!"

At a Canadian charity event held shortly after the awards ceremony, Justin told MuchMusic.com he thought West's interruption put his friend in a tough spot.

"It was her first award, she's 20 years old. I think she didn't deserve to be treated that way."

Taylor and Justin are always sending each other shout-outs on Twitter, and he performed on her United Kingdom tour. Now that Justin has publicly defended her honor, their friendship (they both insist it's nothing more than that) is good as gold.

As he looks to the future, this rookie pop star promises **giving back** will remain one of his **top priorities.**

Justin performs on NBC's *Today* show
in New York City, June 4, 2010.

Showing Chuck Norris Some Love

Justin Bieber calls Chuck Norris his "idol."

Norris, 70, is a martial artist and actor who gained great fame portraying *Walker, Texas Ranger* on CBS from 1993 to 2001. Thanks to his tough-guy image, an Internet phenomenon known as Chuck Norris Facts began in 2005. The "facts" are usually absurd claims about Norris' toughness and masculinity.

Justin has hopped onto the Norris bandwagon in a big way. He's posted videos about the veteran actor and loves to tweet Chuck Norris jokes to his followers:

"Chuck Norris bought *Baby* on iTunes infinity times ... twice."

"**Random Chuck Norris Moment:** Chuck Norris does not style his hair. It lays perfectly in place out of sheer terror."

"**Random Chuck Norris Moment:** Chuck Norris destroyed the periodic table, because Chuck Norris only recognizes the element of surprise."

It should be no surprise, then, that Justin says if there's ever a movie made about his life, he hopes Chuck Norris portrays him – beard, karate kicks and all.

Justin performs during Z100's Jingle Ball 2009 at Madison Square Garden.

JUSTIN

BIEBER

Chapter 6: Not the First Teen Idol

CHAPTER 5:
NOT THE FIRST
TEEN IDOL

Elvis Presley may just be a face you see on postage stamps. You may think of Donny Osmond simply as that guy who was on *Dancing with the Stars*. And you may only know John Travolta as the voice of Disney's lost canine *Bolt*.

The truth is, these are the guys your mom – and grandmother, and maybe even great-grandmother – swooned over when they were teenagers.

That's right, nearly every woman or girl remembers the days of singing along with the radio in her bedroom, holding a hairbrush for a microphone. They remember tearing pictures of cute celebrities out of magazines, covering their bedroom walls with "his" posters, and knowing the words to all "his" songs.

Justin Bieber may be today's hot, new teen idol. But he's certainly not the first teen idol the world has known.

A teen idol is someone – generally a singer or actor – who is widely admired by teens. Some teen idols are teenagers themselves, others are young but not necessarily teens.

Some teen idols mature along with their fan base, to become successful adult musicians or actors. The Beatles, for

(Left) Entertainer Donny Osmond and Kym Johnson from *Dancing With the Stars*. (Right) Actors John Travolta and Olivia Newton-John embrace in a promotional still for the film, *Grease*.

example, were four mop-topped young men who had girls fainting at concerts in the early 1960s. Between 1964 and 1970, a Beatles song occupied the No. 1 spot on Billboard charts for a total of 58 weeks. The group disbanded in 1970 and the four set out on their own successful paths. Only two

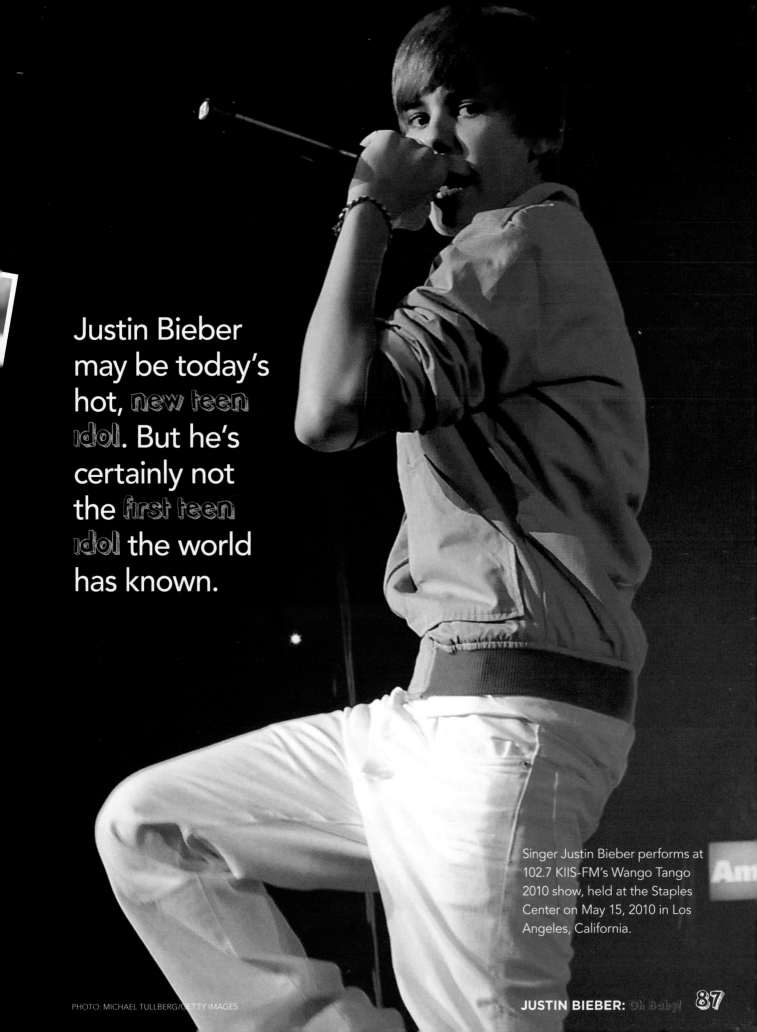

Justin Bieber may be today's hot, new teen idol. But he's certainly not the first teen idol the world has known.

Singer Justin Bieber performs at 102.7 KIIS-FM's Wango Tango 2010 show, held at the Staples Center on May 15, 2010 in Los Angeles, California.

of the band members, Paul McCartney and Ringo Starr, are still alive and performing today. In January 2010 Starr released his 15th studio album, "Y Not," and McCartney is listed in *The Guinness Book of World Records* as the most successful musician and composer in popular music history with sales of 100 million singles and 60 gold records.

Others have enjoyed similar success translating teen adoration into big-time, grown-up stardom.

The Beatles, for example, were four mop-topped young men who had girls fainting at concerts in the early 1960s.

A few who come to mind:

➡ The King of Pop, **Michael Jackson** was a teen idol in the 1980s, as well as in the 1970s, when he was one of the popular Jackson Five.

UNLIKELY FANS

Thirty-five-year-old Spanish pop music singer-songwriter Enrique Iglesias may not fit the profile of the average Justin Bieber fan, but he loves JB nonetheless.

Talking to *PopEater.com*, Iglesias described Justin as a "talented kid."

"He's everywhere. I've heard his music," he said. "I actually like that song he did with Ludacris, 'Baby'. It's hooky. It's a hooky song. I think he's a talented kid."

Even the women who love Enrique Iglesias are jumping on the Justin bandwagon.

Shantel Simpson, a 39-year-old mother of three says she caught Bieber Fever the first time she hit Justin's music on the radio.

"I like Justin's sincerity," she told *PopEater. com*. "He seems really down to Earth, and his mom seems to be doing a good job."

Simpson says Justin has lots of post-high school admirers, but most keep their fandom a secret.

"There are a lot of older fans, but people are just afraid to admit it," she said.

Enrique Iglesias

The Beatles, rock 'n' roll's all-time best-selling act, were a pop-music sensation in the 1960s.

⇨ **Justin Timberlake** has won six Grammys and two Emmys since his days touring with boy-band *N Sync. Even before that, he was part of The Mickey Mouse Club cast.

⇨ Oscar-nominated actor **Mark Wahlberg** is a leading man today. Back in 1991 he was known as rap musician Marky Mark.

⇨ In spring 2010 **Johnny Depp** became the first actor to star in two films that have grossed more than $1 billion each: *Alice in Wonderland* and *Pirates of the Caribbean: Dead Man's Chest*. He first gained stardom in 1987 playing a lead role on Fox TV's *21 Jump Street*.

Of course, not all teen idols are so lucky

David Cassidy, Ralph Macchio, Willie Aames and others were all beloved in their time, yet none of them earned solid crossover appeal in the grown-up market. Sure, some teen idols manage to stay in the business by taking small parts or moving to behind-the-scenes positions. Corey Feldman, for example, starred in 1980s hits *The Goonies*, *Stand By Me* and *The Lost Boys*. These days, he's getting work in straight-to-DVD movies and doing voicing for the animated *Robot Chicken*.

Still others have had a more difficult time dealing with the fading spotlight. Blond, blue-eyed singer/actor Leif Garrett, for example, reigned supreme in the 1970s. In the years since, he's struggled with substance abuse

"You don't want to leave people behind, but it's fair to surprise people or even sometimes scare people a little bit." —Taylor Hanson

COULD A MOVIE BE FAR BEHIND?

Justin Bieber is obviously devoted to his music career, but he's not ruling out trying new things.

In fact, he's already tested his acting jobs a couple times – to rave reviews. He took over the popular comedy website *FunnyOrDie.com* on April Fool's day, joking about his extravagant lifestyle as one of the world's most famous 16-year-olds.

In an April 2010 appearance on NBC's *Saturday Night Live*, he acted in a pair of skits. *Saturday Night Live* executive producer Lorne Michaels told *People* magazine that Justin was "a complete pro" on the show.

Veteran director Garry Marshall is planning a New Year's Eve sequel to his hit movie *Valentine's Day*.

"Already, they're mentioning Justin Bieber," Marshall told *MTV News* about possible casting. "I have no idea who that is, but I'm sure we'll meet."

And Justin's made it no secret that his manager, Scooter Braun, is in negotiations with screenwriters and producers to develop a project for the star.

"We're trying to set up a movie for me in the near future—it's going to be similar to the story of how I got discovered. Kinda like my own version of *8 Mile*," he told *Teen Vogue* in April 2010.

and, in February 2010 he was arrested for the second time in four years for narcotics possession.

So, what's the secret to surviving puberty *and* teen stardom?

Taylor Hanson, who soared to fame in the early 1990s as part of the pop band Hanson and now lead singer for the band Tinted Windows, says the keys are to be involved in the long-term business decisions that affect your career, to become a serious student of vocal technique, and to evolve as you go.

"You don't want to leave people behind, but it's fair to surprise people or even sometimes scare people a little bit," he told *Entertainment Weekly*. "You have to figure out how to evolve, because it has to be interesting to you. When it stops being interesting to you, it'll stop being interesting to everyone else, too."

Music critics are divided on whether Justin will still be churning out hits five, 10, or more years down the road.

Sarah Godfrey writes in the *Washington Post's Click Track* blog that she doubts Justin's ability to make the transition: "He could turn out to be the next Justin Timberlake, forcing me to eat my words, but my gut tells me that he's a blip and that his success is inversely proportional to the amount of facial hair he sprouts.

Could he pull a Bobby Brown and manage to stay relevant into his twenties? Maybe, but he'd need a serious overhaul to make it work. The idea of a 25-year-old Bieber singing "Favorite Girl" in husky tones kind of creeps me out."

The idea of a 25-year-old Bieber singing "Favorite Girl" in husky tones kind of creeps me out. —Sarah Godfrey

True/Slant entertainment contributor Jeremy Helligar says he thinks Justin has the potential to keep churning out hits for years to come. "He writes songs, plays instruments, and he doesn't pretend to be anything he's not. He looks and acts his age. Plus, he's got something teen icons rarely have — street cred."

Washington Post pop music critic Chris Richards thinks Justin has what it takes to become an adult superstar. "… I think Bieber actually has an ear for what great pop music sounds like," he says. "He'll figure out how to use his man-voice accordingly."

Justin performs on the first day of BBC Radio 1's Big Weekend on May 22, 2010, in Bangor, Wales.

PHOTO: SAMIR HUSSEIN/GETTY IMAGES

Pretty Boy

Ask any of the Bieber Legion and they'll tell you Justin is a cutie … but *People* magazine made it official when editors named him to their 2010 list of "100 Most Beautiful People" in the world alongside celebrities including Julia Roberts, Katy Perry and Robert Pattinson.

In a blurb on *People's* website, Justin acknowledges the allure of his trademark hairstyle but adds, "Your hair doesn't make you who you are. It's part of my image; it's not who I am."

Just a month after the *People* list was released, *HELLO! Canada* published its list of "50 Most Beautiful Canadians." And who was gracing the cover of that magazine? None other than young Mr. Bieber!

"Justin is a real cutie," *HELLO!* editor-in-chief Ciara Hunt told Canadian wire services. "As Michael Buble said, 'It's neat to see a young kid taking over the world.' I couldn't agree more."

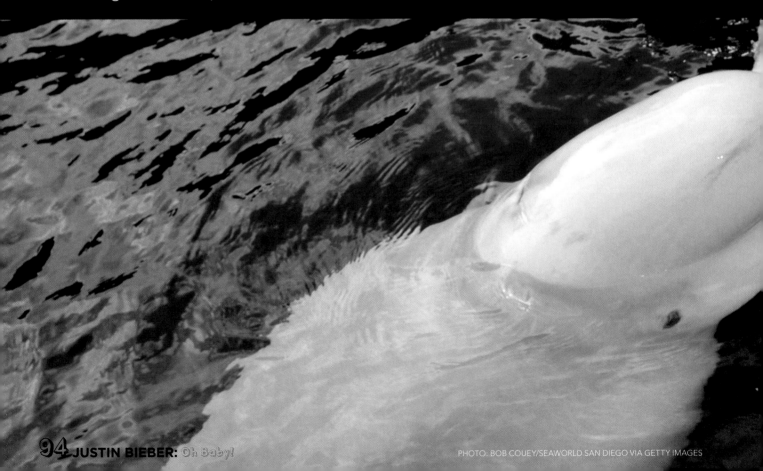

Critics, ladies, other musicians … everyone loves Justin – even Allua, a female beluga whale at San Diego's SeaWorld. Justin stopped by the park in May 2010.

Dream Girls

Justin Bieber says he's not yet been in love, but that doesn't stop him from hanging out with, flirting with, and – yes – kissing the ladies.

Justin tells *Seventeen* magazine he got his first kiss when he was 13 and confesses to *CNN* he has made out with "a couple chicks," adding, "I'm a good – I'm a *great* – kisser."

While his hectic schedule and lack of privacy don't really allow for a long-term relationship right now, he's clearly given some thought to what his ideal girl is like.

"The two qualities she has to have are, one, she has to make me laugh because I like a sense of humor and I like to laugh," he told *Star* magazine. "And, two, I also like a girl who is smart so we can carry on a conversation."

JUSTIN

BIEBER

Epilogue: *My World Tour*

EPILOGUE
MY WORLD TOUR

Swarms of teenage girls have been flocking to arenas in cities across the country – from Hartford, Connecticut, to Tulsa, Oklahoma, – to catch Justin Bieber's first headlining tour. The buzz has been incredible as Justin has dazzled fans with favorites like "Baby," "One Time," and "One Less Lonely Girl."

Of course, moving a show as large as this from one city to another takes a lot of personnel and top-notch coordination. For example, nine trucks and 11 buses are used to transport all the equipment and people from venue to venue. Every worker has a job to do, whether it's loading confetti guns or cleaning costumes, setting up media interviews or managing sound checks. What looks like fun and games for the audience actually requires hours of hard work.

Of course, all work and no play would make Justin a dull boy, so it should be no surprise that the teen idol has found plenty of ways to entertain himself (and others) while on the road.

A throng of young girls in Des Moines, Iowa, for instance, got a cool surprise while waiting outside Justin's tour bus. Armed with water guns and water balloons, Justin and his crew doused the delighted – and very soaked – fans.

In Colorado, Justin spent his downtime playing basketball, even taking time to tweet to his followers: "Been hoopin' all day … ball players in Denver must be in incredible shape because the air is thinner up here."

MY WORLD 2010 TOUR DATES:

Date	City	Date	City	Date	City
6/23	Hartford, Connecticut	7/13	Everett, Washington	8/4	Orlando, Florida
6/24	Trenton, New Jersey	7/14	Portland, Oregon	8/5	Sunrise, Florida
6/26	Cincinnati, Ohio	7/17	Oakland, California	8/8	Charlotte, North Carolina
6/27	Milwaukee, Wisconsin	7/18	Reno, Nevada	8/9	Duluth, Georgia
6/29	Minneapolis, Minnesota	7/20	Los Angeles, California	8/11	Nashville, Tennessee
6/30	Des Moines, Iowa	7/21	Paso Robles, California	8/12	Indianapolis, Indiana
7/2	Moline, Illinois	7/24	Las Vegas, Nevada	8/14	Columbus, Ohio
7/3	Omaha, Nebraska	7/25	Glendale, Arizona	8/15	Auburn Hills, Michigan
7/5	Grand Prairie, Texas	7/28	Kansas City, Missouri	8/21	Toronto, Ontario
7/6	Tulsa, Oklahoma	7/29	N. Little Rock, Arkansas	8/22	London, Ontario
7/8	Broomfield, Colorado	7/31	Memphis, Tennessee	8/24	Ottawa, Ontario
7/10	W. Valley City, Utah	8/1	Lafayette, Louisiana	8/25	Albany, New York

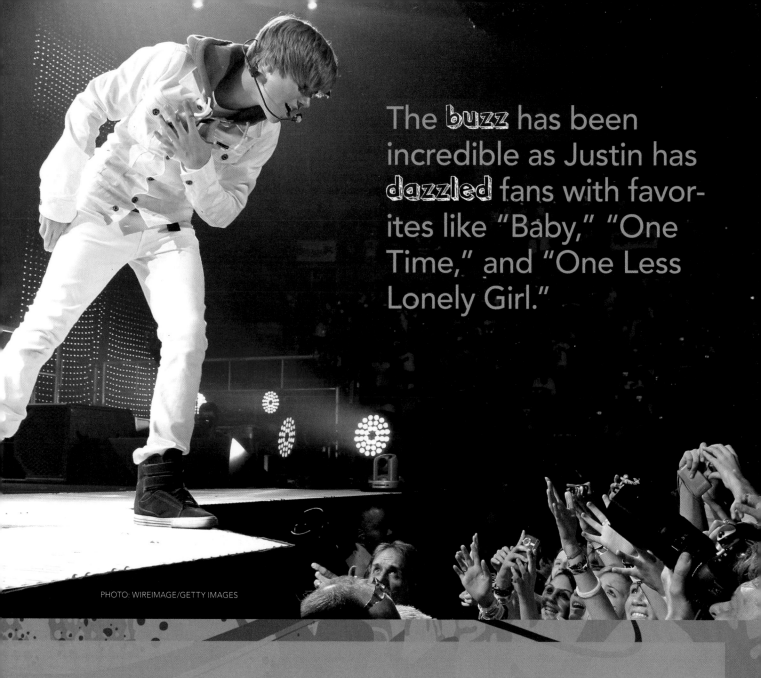

The **buzz** has been incredible as Justin has **dazzled** fans with favorites like "Baby," "One Time," and "One Less Lonely Girl."

PHOTO: WIREIMAGE/GETTY IMAGES

8/27	Providence, Rhode Island	10/22	Sacramento, California	11/16	Boston, Massachusetts
8/28	Newark, New Jersey	10/24	Ontario, California	11/17	East Rutherford, New Jersey
8/29	Syracuse, New York	10/25	Los Angeles, California	11/20	Atlantic City, New Jersey
8/31	New York, New York	10/27	Anaheim, California	11/22	Montreal, Quebec
9/1	Manchester, New Hampshire	10/28	San Jose, California	11/23	Toronto, Ontario
9/3	Essex Junction, Vermont	10/30	San Diego, California	12/13	Pittsburgh, Pennsylvania
9/4	Allentown, Pennsylvania	11/3	Oklahoma City, Oklahoma	12/15	Greensboro, North Carolina
9/5	Timonium, Maryland	11/5	San Antonio, Texas	12/16	Greenville, South Carolina
9/14	Winnipeg, Manitoba	11/6	Houston, Texas	12/18	Miami, Florida
9/16	Regina, Saskatchewan	11/8	St. Louis, Missouri	12/19	Tampa, Florida
9/17	Saskatoon, Saskatchewan	11/10	Louisville, Kentucky	12/21	Birmingham, Alabama
9/19	Edmonton, Alberta	11/11	Cleveland, Ohio	12/23	Atlanta, Georgia
9/20	Calgary, Alberta	11/13	Norfolk, Virginia		
10/19	Vancouver, British Columbia	11/14	Philadelphia, Pennsylvania		

MEET OPENING ACT JESSICA JARRELL

Think you recognize Jessica Jarrell, one of the opening acts on Justin Bieber's *My World* Tour?

That could be because the 15-year-old Los Angeles native is the bluesy female voice on Justin's ballad "Overboard" from *My World 2.0.*

In addition to opening for the first leg of Justin's tour, Jarrell also makes an appearance during his set to perform their duet.

"I come out during his set and there's a bunch of fog on the stairs," she told *MTV News.* "I'm excited about that song. It's a lot of fun. We goof off and have a great time... It sounds great to be in an arena. It all sounds really good, the whole show, the lighting, everything."

While Justin tweeted about pre-tour jitters, Jarrell said the June 23 kickoff show in Hartford, Connecticut, gave her a "rush."

"I was a little nervous earlier," she told *MTV News.* "I was like, 'Oh my God! There's going to be so many people,' but you know I'm really excited. It's overwhelming, but it's a lot of fun to be able to look out and see all of those girls screaming. It's just crazy!

You get an adrenaline rush!"

Mercury Records/Teen Island's newest star set off on Justin's tour just as her single "Up and Running" hit pop and rhythm radio formats across the country. Her debut album, most of which she co-wrote, is forthcoming.

Jarrell's first single, "Armageddon," became a Billboard Top 5 dance hit.

"(The song is) all about that one guy every girl dates who she needs to just cut off but just can't bring herself to do it," she said in her official Mercury Records biography. "I can't date until I'm 16, but I still like boys and have watched my friends go through break-ups, so I used that as inspiration."

Jarrell's career started more than a decade ago; she was just four years old when she was featured in print campaigns for major brands, including K-Mart, American Girl, and Mattel. When she was 11, her friends dragged her to the audition for their school's Christmas play.

"We went for fun, so I auditioned for one solo part and ended up getting two," she said. "My mom was shocked. She came to rehearsals and cried when she heard me."

After performing in front of her school, Jarrell was hooked on the rush of being on stage.

"To be honest, I always loved to sing," she said, "I was just too shy to sing anywhere other than in the shower!"

That's a case of stage fright she's clearly kicked.

And in Omaha, Justin and his tour buddies spent some of their free time at an Omaha mall, where they bought tennis shoes and wrote an impromptu rap they called "Omaha Mall" – a song that likely won't make his next album.

Singing the same songs in the same order every night could become boring, but Justin is determined to keep his tour fresh and fun. His crew and fellow performers know that means they better watch out because "fun" often means being pranked by Justin; shaving cream and hot-sauce attacks keep everyone on their toes.

Immature? Maybe. But in Justin's case, that's OK.

"I'm only 16 once," he says. "I've got to live like it."

"I'm only 16 once," he says. "I've got to live like it."

HOW IT ALL ADDS UP

Justin Bieber + Teen Girls = Mass Hysteria

That's a mathematical equation with which you just can't argue. What other numerical statistics do we know about Justin?

1: Number of 2010 Teen Choice award nominations he received.

4: The number of Top 40 singles he had before the release of his debut album.

5: The number of minutes he says he spends styling his hair each day.

8: The age at which he started playing the guitar.

10: Average number of tweets Justin sends out each day.

10: Number of countries where Justin's debut single "One Time" charted in the Top 30.

27: Average number of dollars spent per person on merchandise at each stop on Justin's North American tour.

56: Number of times the word "baby" is sung in Justin's single "Baby."

76: Number of stops on his *My World* Tour.

2,000,000: Number of copies of *My World 2.0* sold by mid-2010.

PHOTO: (TOP) ABC VIA GETTY IMAGES, (BOTTOM) ASSOCIATED PRESS

Tweets from the Road

As of May 2010 Justin had more than 2.7 million followers on Twitter, making him one of the most-followed people on the service.

Justin's manager, Scooter Braun, says Justin spends about two hours each day on Twitter. Speaking to an audience at a 2010 technology conference in New York, Braun said the service is pretty important. For instance, if he responds to a post from a girl who thought she'd never talk to Justin, "That's something she'll remember for the rest of her life."

Incredible show last night. Tulsa has always been good to me. First place to play ONE TIME in the states.
10:07 A.M., JULY 7, 2010

SOUNDCHECK and a game of HORSE as a warmup...this is what we do in crappy weather... someone bring the sunshine.
3:25 P.M., JULY 6, 2010

big bro @seankingston just got off stage. He is right...it's a blessing 2 share our music every night with these incredible fans. A blessing.
6:22 P.M., JULY 3, 2010

I legit have the best job in the world! seeing all those smiles out there 2nite...thanks 2 every1 who came out. hope u enjoyed it like i did.
10:26 P.M., JULY 2, 2010

MN thanks 4 an incredible night...and those fans who were witness to the #EpicWaterFight .... no worries... #TeamBieber will seek our revenge.
10:44 P.M., JUNE 29, 2010

Rolled into Milwaukee for the show today...gonna be huge...22,000 people sold out i heard. Missing everybody out in LA for the BET awards.
10:31 A.M., JUNE 27, 2010

Got to sleep in....feeling good....taking a day off...relaxin on the water. gonna go WAKE BOARDING!!! haha. good times.
9:00 A.M., JUNE 25, 2010

Went to sleep on the bus and woke up in a different state ready for a new show. The party on wheels dominates once again.
9:43 A.M., JUNE 24, 2010

Kinda nervous and hyped right now. today is the 1st day of the MY WORLD TOUR!! We still have a lot to do.
6:34 A.M., JUNE 23, 2010

WALK THIS WAY

Sure, Justin performs his own music during his *My World* Tour, but he also rocks out on a couple covers. One of the more notable covers is Aerosmith's "Walk This Way." Aerosmith is the best-selling American rock band of all time and holds the record for the most gold and multi-platinum albums by an American group.

Written by Steven Tyler and Joe Perry, "Walk this Way" peaked at No. 10 on the Billboard Hot 100 in 1977.

> ## Written by Steven Tyler and Joe Perry, "Walk this Way" peaked at No. 10 on the Billboard Hot 100 in 1977.

The song has been recorded by others throughout the years, most notably by Run D.M.C. in 1986 on their album *Raising Hell*. The rappers made the song an international hit and it earned them a Soul Train Music Award in 1987.

"Walk this Way" is included on the list of the Rock and Roll Hall of Fame's "500 Songs that Shaped Rock and Roll."

During Justin's performance of the song, fans get a chance to see their musical idol take a turn on the drums. Rock on!

IT'S A HOT, HOT TICKET!

Justin Bieber's July 5, 2010, concert in Grand Prairie, Texas, sold out in just 13 seconds. Tickets for his September 16 show at the Brandt Centre in Regina, Saskatchewan, Canada, went on sale in June; the concert sold out in 49 minutes. And so it's gone in city after city, as Justin and his crew have weaved their way across North America.

Justin has had no problem packing shows at a time when ticket sales for big arena tours in North America are suffering industry-wide.

For the first six months of 2010, combined ticket sales for big concerts like AC/DC and the Jonas Brothers have dropped to their lowest level since 2005. The industry magazine *Pollster* reported that gross revenues for the top 100 Tours in North America are down nearly $200 million from the same period in 2009.

With tickets to Justin's shows in such high demand, it should be no surprise that once shows sell out, resellers are charging as much as $3,000 for a single VIP ticket (which includes a floor seat, entry to preshow soundcheck and party, gift bag, and autographed book or program).

NO NORTH KOREA STOP FOR THIS TOUR

Poor Justin. According to recent Internet hoaxes, his mom is posing for *Playboy* magazine, he's been arrested in Texas, and he died – more than once.

At this point, he's probably getting used to all the rumors and pranks, but there's a hoax about his debut tour that won't seem to go away.

It started with a fake contest run by a website called Faxo.com. The contest encouraged fans to vote for the country they wanted Justin to visit on an upcoming leg of his *My World* Tour. There were no restrictions or limitations – they could vote for any country.

With encouragement from the jokesters at the 4chan message board, thousands of votes were cast for North Korea – a country with virtually no Internet access and a government that blocks outside media and pop culture influences.

A spokesperson for Justin set the record straight in an email to *MTV News*: "It was a spoof site. This is not a legitimate contest."

Good thing Justin seems to be handling all this craziness with a sense of humor.

"Let's take some time to answer some crazy (rumors) … I'm not dead," he tweeted to fans in June 2010. "I had to check on this one … but it turns out I'm alive."

JUSTIN & SEAN:
FRIENDS, JOKESTERS, COLLABORATORS

As Justin Bieber's *My World* Tour zigzags its way across North America, his pal Sean Kingston will be there, right beside him.

Rapper Kingston is one of the opening acts on the first leg of the tour; he also joins Justin during his set to perform "Eenie Meenie."

Kingston meet Justin in 2009 at a radio show; the two quickly became friends.

"I'm kind of like his big brother," says Kingston, who helped Justin celebrate his 16th birthday in Los Angeles. The two singers share a love of sneakers, practical jokes, fast cars, X-Box games and, of course, music.

They say their collaboration on "Eenie Meenie" is just the beginning.

"We're starting a writing team together," Kingston told *All Music Guide.*

Kingston was born in Miami, Florida, and raised in Kingston, Jamaica. His real name is Kisean Anderson; his stage name honors his adopted homeland.

Kingston's island upbringing is obvious in the way he weaves reggae beats into his hip-hop stylings. His lyrics reflect an often-difficult life. He has been homeless, his mother served time in jail, and at age 11 he was incarcerated for breaking and entering.

As a teen, he decided to channel his energies into more productive things. Relying on his ability to write rhymes and hooks, he moved back to Miami and started working the city's talent show circuit. He performed in tiny clubs, then larger ones, until finally he was sharing the stage with artists including Pitbull, Ludacris, and Trick Daddy.

Producer Jonathan "J.R." Rotem, who has worked with artists including Rihanna, 50 Cent, Lil' Kim and Britney Spears, heard Kingston's demo and immediately was smitten. Rotem signed Kingston to Epic Records under his Beluga Heights label.

Kingston's single "Colors 2007" – featuring The Game and Rick Ross – was released in 2007, when Kingston was just 16 years old. His second single, "Beautiful Girls," sampled Ben E. King's "Stand by Me" and rose to hit status; it was No. 1 on the U.S. Billboard singles chart for three weeks.

On the heels of his newfound fame, Kingston became the opening act for Gwen Stefani's *The Sweet Escape* Tour and performed select dates on Beyonce's *The Beyonce Experience* Tour.

"Music has just always been a part of me, period," he told *MTV News*, noting his grandfather, Jack Ruby, was a well-known music producer in Jamaica.

"He did a lot of stuff for Bob Marley, Burning Spear, Buju Banton and all these big dudes. And I feel like he inspired me when I (would) go to Jamaica and I'd just go in the studio with him and we'd just vibe out and I'd see how he created music in the culture, in Jamaica."

In addition to being featured on Justin's album, "Eenie Meenie" is the lead single on Kingston's third album, which is expected to be released in late 2010.

JUSTIN BIEBER: Oh Baby!

The Reviews Are In ...

Teens, tweens and their parents have flocked to Justin's My World Tour, sometimes shelling out more than more than $3,000 to buy a single VIP ticket from a reseller.

The fans clearly love him, but what have the nation's music critics had to say about Justin's first-ever North American tour? Here are excerpts from some of his earliest reviews.

"He sang tunefully and with feeling on the slower numbers, though his voice sometimes sounded raspy, as though he was suffering from allergies. Or puberty. Either way, he often sang along with recorded tracks, which resulted in an opening-night glitch when they seemed to drop out on 'Runaway Love.'"

Eric R. Danton in the *Hartford Courant*, June 23, 2010

"And for 90 minutes, the rehashed puppy-love pop-song style that can be charming in a single three-minute dose, becomes as sustained and annoying as the hum of a vuvuzela, and preteen screaming couldn't even drown it out."

Chris Varias in the *Cincinnati Enquirer*, June 27, 2010

"As a lite-soul/teen-pop stylist, he's light years better than Aaron Carter, but a little less evolved musically than the Jonas Brothers."

Dave Tianen in the *Milwaukee Journal Sentinel*, June 28, 2010

"He is a little daredevil. He flew over the main floor, first in a heart-shaped frame (sitting in a chair, playing an acoustic guitar, performing without his band) and later in a metal basket modeled after a hot-air balloon basket (singing with the band). And, wearing a harness, he even faux-climbed up a wall to spray-paint his graffiti tag. This was a smartly executed production."

Jon Bream in the *Minneapolis Star Tribune*, June 30, 2010

"… Bieber's handlers put more effort than one might expect into the stage production, essentially designing a show that gave the crowd endless amounts of face time with Bieber, while throwing in just enough lasers and fog to keep dads in the audience from falling asleep. (If, indeed, it was possible to snooze in the middle of an ocean of jet engine-like squealing.)"

Ross Raihala in the *St. Paul Pioneer Press*, June 30, 2010

"Bieber's voice was impressive throughout his set – during 'You Smile,' his high tenor was clear, nimble, and on pitch. Synchronized dance moves didn't affect his voice in 'Somebody to Love.'"

Sophia Ahma d in the *Des Moines Register*, July 1, 2010

"Bieber is close to mastering the panache of a showman. He knows just what his young crowd wants, and is willing to give it to them in songs about lonely, smiling girls who long to have their hands held. He was backed by a six-man rock/R&B band and four energetic breakdancers."

David Burke in the *Quad-City Times*, July 2, 2010

"At times, the teen was nearly dwarfed by over-the-top production and well-placed and well-rehearsed monologues, but nothing could completely mask the flex of his Michael Jackson-esque vocal muscle."

Jennifer Chancellor in the *Tulsa Tribune*, July 7, 2010

I like a girl who is smart
so we can carry on a
conversation.